Hope in Brokenness

Finding Healing in Christ Amidst Broken Families

A 16-day devotional discovering hope within family brokenness in your life and in the lives around you

Jordan Mancl

Contents

Preface

The topic of family brokenness can be broad and the effects can greatly vary. I publish this devotional having been personally impacted by the brokenness within my own family. I would have never decided to write this unless I saw in myself and others the domino effect of residual sin as a result of broken homes. It affects relationships with peers, trust with authority figures, sexuality, emotional swings of anger and jealousy, conflict issues, mental health struggles, suicidal ideation, and more.

While both of my parents loved us siblings, they divorced before my first memories. I grew up in two households with parents who had a consistently adversarial relationship. I knew something was off as a child, but this struggle was the only normal I had ever experienced.

Normal childhood for me was having two different parental value systems and standards applied to two separate households. I tried to appease both parent's ideals and expectations, which consumed much of my efforts through my adolescent and teen years. Freshman year of high school, my mom and stepdad moved to Ohio, many hours from my dad and stepmom back in Wisconsin. While this was a painful separation, something deep within me quietly yearned for it. For the first time in my life, I would be living in one household every day of the week, which was a foreign and desirable concept to me. This might sound odd, but for someone who spent every weekend and every other weekday at a different house, this provided a semblance of stability for a brief time during my teenage years.

My life was changed forever by two very different events. The first was trusting Jesus as my Lord and Savior in elementary school through the efforts of my local church and also my dad, who came to know God personally just a few years earlier. The second was junior year of high school when my mom suffered a brain aneurysm that took her life. This obviously was a shocking and chaotic time within our family. Not only did I lose my mom, but now my sister and I were moving back to Wisconsin for my last year of high school. At this point, I wanted nothing more than to go to college and leave this family drama and brokenness I had no control over.

Little did I know that hardship and residual effects would follow me for years to come. I thought the past would have little effect on the future, but I was wrong. The effects from my broken past damaged relationships and myself. There are no magic buttons to seek healing and forgiveness, rather, it has been a long journey of seeking the Lord and others for wisdom and guidance. It would have been much easier to suppress the past and not address these issues, but that wouldn't be seeking the Lord's transformative work in my life and my family's. Instead, it might be carrying and passing brokenness to those around me while not living the abundant and transformed life God desires.

My hope and prayer with this devotional is for those from broken homes to find reflective healing in Christ while those from lesser family brokenness might show deeper understanding and love to those around them who come from situations of immense brokenness.

Introduction

Why are Broken Families Rarely Addressed?

I've wondered over the years why I don't see many books, talks, or a general focus on brokenness within families. You certainly don't have to search far to find books on prayer, evangelism, marriage, discipleship, or missions. I've been hard-pressed, however, to find a sufficient number of helpful resources on understanding and navigating the struggles of broken homes. I would argue that many unhealthy patterns easily stem from broken households. Some of these patterns could include a lack of trust in peers and authority figures, sexual struggles, boundary issues with the opposite gender, struggles to grow close to others, lack of vulnerability, unjustified anger, and a wide range of others. Those in Christian circles may be acutely aware on how to manage the surface effects, but fail to address the root issues from a broken past.

Now I understand there may be many ways to define a broken family. It's hard to establish a good definition since modern culture tends to frequently redefine the standards for a healthy family. For the sake of this devotion, we will focus on what are termed *primary* and *secondary* broken family situations. A primary broken home would be a family with extremely severed ties in relationships, such as unexpected death, divorce, or disowning. The severed ties in a primary broken family are clear and obvious from an outside observer. Conversely, there are situations of family brokenness that can be labeled as secondary. These situations are subtler and also include severed relationships related to mental health problems, physical/sexual/ emotional abuse, financial difficulties or success, a major difference in beliefs or values, disabilities, a disrespect of boundaries, etc. These issues of brokenness are not less important, rather, they are subtler to an outside observer. It may appear that a family is functioning well, yet relationships are affected within. While the issues of primary and secondary brokenness aren't more or less important than the other, the residual impact between the two can be vastly different, especially from a primary broken home. This is why not all broken family situations should be treated as equal or comparable to each other.

Why is the topic of broken families rarely discussed?

There could be many reasons this topic isn't discussed often, but here are a few reasons I've observed.

1. A person may not grasp the impact for years to come

Most adolescents, teenagers, and young adults who grew up in broken homes don't think about the residual impacts until years later, if ever. There are obviously exceptions to this, but my experience in working with college students from broken homes, most don't make the connection between the residual effects they experience today and their broken past. I once even had a young adult give a loud assertion, "I don't see how my broken family affects my future!"

For many, including myself, a broken home is simply normal because that's all we knew. Think about this: How is a child supposed to fully understand what a healthy family looks like if they haven't experienced it in their developmental stages? Have you ever observed another family and immediately recognize areas of brokenness from your vantage point? Chances are, these areas of brokenness appear normal to that family because that is simply what they've been accustomed to.

2. It's a delicate topic

Often, when sin is addressed in western culture, it is viewed from an individualistic perspective. We are reluctant to address and recognize collective sin. Scripture is full of examples of collective sin of families and nations. Brokenness within families can be challenging because it often involves wrongdoing by one or several individuals who affect the unit as a whole.

Addressing this collective sin within families can be such a fragile situation because often there is still a bond that exists between relatives. Family members might feel betrayed or offended when past brokenness is resurfaced, especially if it still greatly affects victims but not the perpetrators. Parents who divorce, yet have no experience of divorce with their family might never understand or even want to understand the impact their broken family has on their children. Some family members honestly believe the best way to deal with past brokenness is to ignore it and hope time will heal broken wounds. Children of these broken homes, who are now adults, must tread delicately to seek healing from past wounds while also desiring to respect and honor their family.

Family brokenness is also a delicate topic because it forces a person or family to admit that there is something wrong. Nobody wants to be confronted with their wrongs, especially with an intimate topic like family. Too often people may avoid the topic so there isn't a level of shame placed on others or themselves.

Can you see how it's much easier to give a talk or write a book on standard topics like prayer, discipleship, or evangelism rather than unpack a deeply interpersonal topic potentially full of relational landmines?

The Bible is full of family brokenness. Situations such as sibling rivalry, favoritism, rebellious children, marital difficulties, sexual brokenness, and permanent separation that affected many families, including the lineage that led to the birth of Jesus Christ.

I hope this devotional gives hope for those who have gone through family brokenness. For those who have experience lesser brokenness, my prayer is for loving and understanding others who have experienced a broken home. <u>The good news is that Jesus Christ provides hope and reconciliation to your life and family now, not just in the afterlife</u>.

Each section includes a daily dive into an area of brokenness that has affected you or someone you know. Each day has scripture reading on the topic, a short devotional, how Christ provides hope, and self-reflection which includes an exercise or reflection questions.

> Please resist the temptation to skip ahead to the topic of family brokenness you've experienced. Remember, the journey of faith is not an individual pursuit, but a journey together with other believers. You likely know people who struggle with every one of these areas of brokenness and you might benefit by understanding their situation.

Day 1

Family Patterns: Inherited Brokenness

Read: Exodus 20:4-6, 34:1-9, Romans 8:1, 2 Corinthians 5:17-19

Have you ever met a family who seemed to have sin patterns resurfacing in each generation? It may be alcoholism, favoritism, boundary issues, sexual promiscuity, divorce, or others which may go unnoticed by many within that family.

Now have you thought critically about the unhealthy patterns an outsider might observe in your family? I don't ask this to cause paranoia. Rather, I ask because there may be sinful patterns handed down through your family that you might be subconsciously unaware of.

The patriarchs of our faith didn't fare any better. Take Abraham, known as the father of many nations. Three major world religions claim ties to him. Yet, his family was full of unhealthy habits flowing through the generations.

In fact, generational sin is a pattern scripture warns us about. During the Ten Commandments discourse, God says in Exodus 20:4-6:

> *You shall not make for yourself an idol, or any likeness of what is in heaven above or on the earth beneath or in the water under the earth. You **shall not worship them or serve them; for I, the LORD your God, am a jealous God, visiting the iniquity of** the fathers on the children, on the third and the fourth generations of those who hate Me, but showing*

> *loving kindness to thousands, to those who love Me and keep My commandments.*

This seems unfair to think the sin of our parents and grandparents would affect us. But this is how brokenness works. Brokenness is intertwined with the community around us. Don't get me wrong, we are ultimately punished and judged for our own sin, not the sins of our fathers (Ezekiel 18:19-20). However, the temptations and effects of the sin of our family greatly impacts us, whether we are aware or not.

What was the generational sin Abraham's family endured? There were certainly many, deception being one of them. Abraham lied to Pharaoh about Sarah not being his wife to protect himself in Genesis 12. Isaac lied to the men of Gerar in Genesis 26 and said his wife Rebekah was actually his sister to protect himself as well. Jacob and his mother deceived Isaac into thinking that Jacob was Esau in order to ensure the first-born blessing in Genesis 27. Jacob's kids then deceived their father into thinking Joseph had been killed by wild animals while they sold him into slavery in Genesis 37. Deception was a family trait.

Another generational sin was favoritism. Abraham and Sarah clearly favored Isaac over his half-brother, Ishmael. Isaac favored his son Esau over Jacob, not necessarily because he was the first-born of the twins, but because Esau was a skilled hunter and Isaac loved the wild game Esau produced (Genesis 25:28). Isaac's wife, Rebekah, favored Jacob. Jacob clearly had a favorite child in Joseph as made clear in popular culture by the richly ornamented robe Jacob gave him (Genesis 37:3). Much residual effects resulted from the favoritism each generation displayed.

What are some generational sin patterns displayed in your family? How have they come to fruition in your life? Have you asked outsiders to shed light on patterns of sin that exist in your family?

Hope. The beautiful thing about hope in God is we are not destined for generational curses. Exodus 20:5b-6 gives hope for generational sin:

> *for I, the LORD your God, am a jealous God, visiting the iniquity of the fathers on the children, on the third and the fourth generations of those who hate me, but showing loving kindness to thousands, to those who love me and keep my commandments.*

God desires for us to break generational curses so He may show His loving kindness. Faith in Christ has the power to break these generational curses, as we are now new creations and the old way of brokenness is gone.

We might be the ones who breaks it. It may not happen overnight, though. This is why following Jesus can be difficult, yet abundant. If we want to truly see healing in our lives, we must enter the dirty work of letting go of ourselves so God's restoration is done in our lives.

Next steps. Perhaps you know the generational curses to break in order to move toward a healthy family life God desires. However, you might not know all of them or you may be clueless as to which sinful patterns have developed through the generations. Either is an okay position to be in as long as you are committed to God's transformation in your life and hopefully, your family's lives as well.

If you don't know where to start, putting together a family genogram is one practical way to discover some of these curses (and blessings). This will allow you to see which patterns have made their way through generations. These patterns could be passivity, sexual struggles, faithlessness, poor conflict skills, emotional detachment, boundary struggles, substance abuse, or others.

Below is a QR code leading to a full genogram with a genogram chart on page 14. There are also reflection questions to help discover patterns within your family. I encourage you to fill out a family genogram chart to address the generational sin existing in your family. Allow God to transform you, and prayerfully, your family as well.

Scan to read more about a Family Genogram and go through the process of discovering overt and covert generational sins and habits within your own family.

*Free Genogram Workbook PDF and genogram chart provided by EmotionalHealthy.org

1. When you think about the concept of generational curses (and blessings), what thoughts come to mind?

____

____

____

2. What are some sinful patterns you have seen in your family members throughout the generations?

____

____

____

3. When you look at patterns through the generations, what are some generational blessings?

____

____

____

4. What are the major events (both good and bad) that have shaped your life or your parent's lives?

____

____

____

5. Have you considered asking a trusted peer to give some insight into the sinful patterns they observe in your family?

____

____

____

6. Are there relationships within the family that have experienced severed ties? What have the implications been for the rest of the family?

____

____

____

7. If you are a Christ follower, what are the unhealthy patterns in your family that you are not letting God break or transform with you?

____

____

____

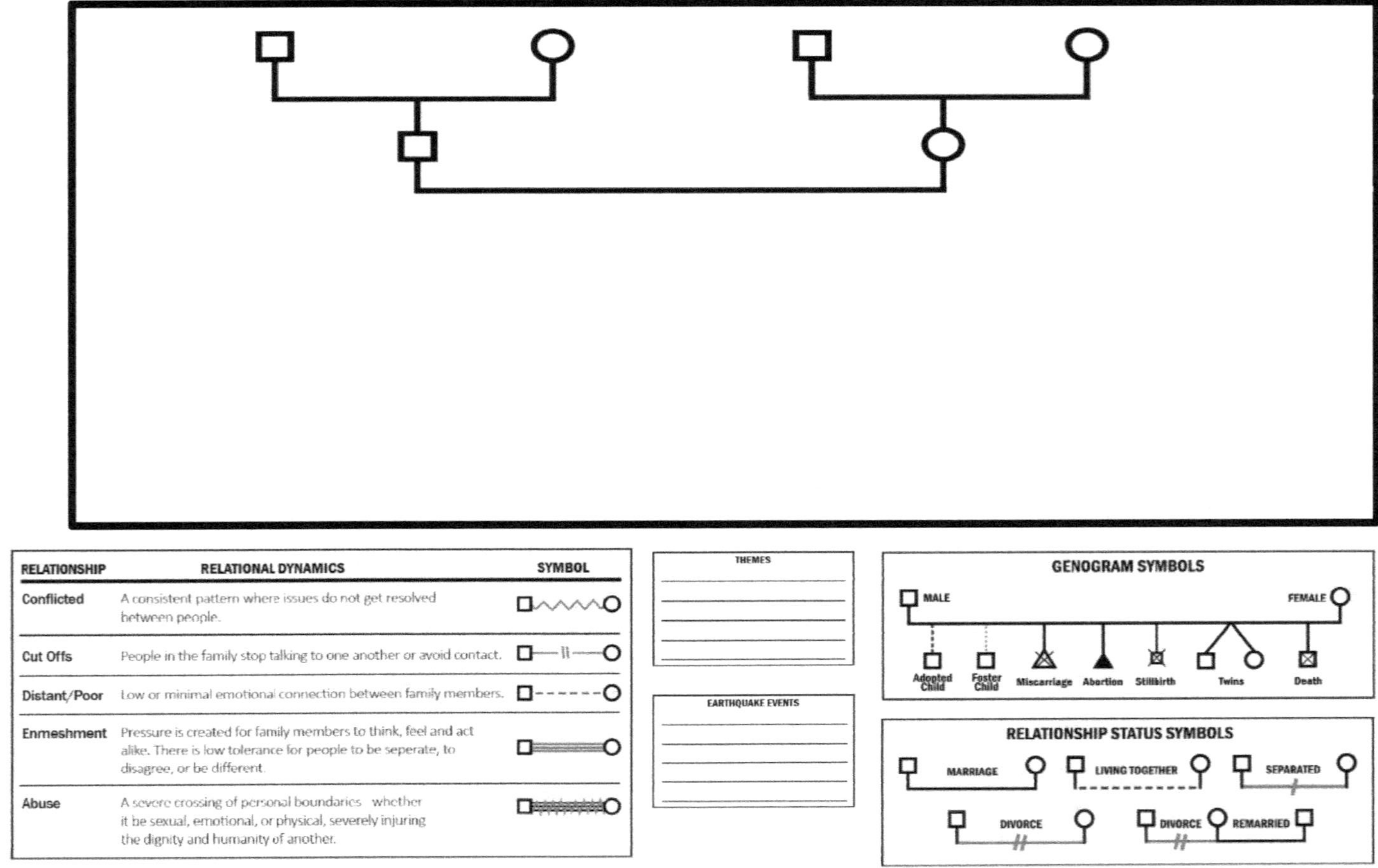

RELATIONSHIP	RELATIONAL DYNAMICS	SYMBOL
Conflicted	A consistent pattern where issues do not get resolved between people.	
Cut Offs	People in the family stop talking to one another or avoid contact.	
Distant/Poor	Low or minimal emotional connection between family members.	
Enmeshment	Pressure is created for family members to think, feel and act alike. There is low tolerance for people to be seperate, to disagree, or be different.	
Abuse	A severe crossing of personal boundaries whether it be sexual, emotional, or physical, severely injuring the dignity and humanity of another.	

Day 2

Sibling Rivalry: Competition and Animosity

Read: Genesis 4

Have you ever encountered a family with siblings who competed with each other? Maybe such rivalry exists between you and your siblings. Sometimes, it may just be childhood competition, but sibling rivalry can blossom well into adult years. I've experienced extended relatives who are siblings, where rivalry or animosity became so massive, they no longer speak to each other. Sometimes the original offense has been so petty, yet animosity between siblings snowballed into a massive or permanent divide.

The first siblings in the history of the world experienced sibling rivalry to the point that one brother killed the other. Genesis 3 records the Fall, when sin and death entered the world. Immediately following, Genesis 4 records the story of Cain and Abel. Both gave offerings to the Lord. God looked upon one of them with favor and one without. We don't fully know why one sacrifice was accepted and the other wasn't, but 1 John 3:12 sheds some light by indicating Cain's deeds had been evil while Abel's were righteous. Cain's competitive jealousy eventually leads him to kill his brother.

Most of us will never get into a heated sibling exchange leading to the murder of a brother or sister. However, the same seed of discord can grow within siblings. Sibling rivalry could subtly move closer to permanent separation, as was the case with other pairs of biblical brothers, Isaac and

Ishmael, and later, Jacob and Esau. It could also lead to betrayal, as was the case with Joseph and his brothers.

Hope. Hope is not lost on sibling rivalry. Despite God punishing Cain, he also marks him to ensure nobody kills him (Gen 4:15-16), thereby graciously delaying judgment he deserved. Ultimately, we do not know if Cain shifted his disposition toward God and others.

God's desire is for the restoration of all things, including family relationships. While Cain and Abel could never be reunited in this world, Jacob and Esau are an example of siblings reunited after a terrible separation. Jacob even believed Esau was going to kill him! Jacob had deceived and stolen the first-born blessing from Esau, which carried enormous family significance in this culture. Esau was obviously furious and the brothers separated with Jacob fearing retaliation from Esau. We don't know what initiated Esau and Jacob moving toward each other. Perhaps the time of separation greatly eased the rivalry, maybe they recognized the importance of a healthy relationship for the sake of their family, or perhaps God was divinely orchestrating this reunion.

Next steps. Where do you stand with your siblings? Are there arguments or disagreements that have snowballed into discord? Here are some reflection questions to shed light into your relationship with your siblings:

1. Are your actions with your sibling(s) pushing you toward a loving relationship or seeking to divide?

   ____

   ____

   ____

2. When making decisions in life, do you spend large amounts of time strategizing and showing how you can do better than a sibling?

   ____

   ____

   ____

3. When you speak of your siblings to others, what is your tone? Do you represent them well in front of others?

   ____

   ____

   ____

4. When you think of academics, sports, fitness, looks, financial well-being, kid's accomplishments, job title, religious activity, or any other idol, are you trying to make sure you are ahead of your siblings?

   ____

   ____

   ____

5. As a parent, is there animosity, bitterness, or quarrels between your children? Are there measures you can take to prevent sibling rivalry?

   ____

   ____

   ____

6. If a sibling were to reach a goal or gain a hard-earned accomplishment, would you celebrate with them?

   ____

   ____

   ____

Day 3

Bad Parenting: The Brokenness from Caregivers

Read: Exodus 20:12, Ephesians 6:1-4, Proverbs 22:15, Matthew 6:9-15, Colossians 3:13

Most people, no matter how much dysfunction in their family, can claim they had parents who loved them. There are situations, unfortunately, when parents don't have their kid's interests at heart, which is an unfortunate occurrence plaguing some families.

King Ahaz, Eli (priest at Shiloh), Lot, even King David could all be labeled as poor parents. Some of these characters not only turned away from God, but also neglected or were largely absent in their children's lives.

King David spent much time on the battlefield and had many wives while fathering at least 20 children. His son Amnon raped his half-sister Tamar, his son Absalom killed Amnon and tried to overthrow David's throne, and another son Adonijah also tried to overthrow David. Rather than instill much needed discipline, it seems like David would rather be furious over his son's actions than provide long-term direction for his children. Even though David was labeled as "a man after God's own heart", he was a preoccupied and absent father to many of his children.

Eli was a priest at Shiloh, where the ark and tabernacle were located. He had two evil sons who he allowed to handle sacrifices, yet they took the meat for themselves that wasn't designated for them and had sex with women in the tabernacle. Eli seemed to passively allow this to continue until judgment came upon them in 1 Samuel 2:22-25:

> *Now Eli, who was very old, heard about everything his sons were doing to all Israel and how they slept with the women who served at the entrance to the tent of meeting. So he said to them, "Why do you do such things? I hear from all the people about these wicked deeds of yours. No, my sons; the report I hear spreading among the LORD's people is not good. If one person sins against another, God may mediate for the offender; but if anyone sins against the LORD, who will intercede for them?" His sons, however, did not listen to their father's rebuke, for it was the LORD's will to put them to death.*

Rather than properly disciplining them as they grew into adulthood, he rebuked them long after their behavior had conjured God's judgement.

Lot provided hospitality for two guests and while staying at his house, a gathering of evil men demanded to have sex with these messengers. Instead, Lot does the unthinkable and sends his two virgin daughters out to satisfy the mob (Genesis 19:8). We don't know what happened with the daughters, but the men seemed to not be interested in them. This story takes place in the greater narrative of the destruction of Sodom and Gomorrah. Lot was willing to abandon the protection of his daughters for the sake of his reputation.

King Ahaz may have been the worst of all biblical parents. Not only did he abandon the Lord and turned to idols, but he also sacrificed his sons in fire to a god of the Ammonites and Canaanites, Molech (2 Kings 16:3, 2 Chronicles 28:3). I don't think anyone needs to be convinced of the bad parenting King Ahaz displays.

Hope. I think many of these biblical examples show a variance of bad parenting that can exist and its effects on their children. The Fall left a trail of brokenness in varying degrees among the institution of families throughout history.

You may be a parent thinking about the influence on your kids or you may be a son or daughter thinking about the influence your parents had on you. No doubt if you are reading this, your desire is the same spirit of Joshua 24:15:

> *"But as for me and my household, we will serve the LORD."*

If you are someone whose parents had such a negative impact on you that will affect the rest of your life, I join with many others in the church in your grief and sorrow. Even if reconciliation never comes with you and your parents, hear this and hold firm to God's character in Psalm 27:10:

> *Even if my father and mother abandon me, the LORD will hold me close.*

Next steps. There are no quick and easy fixes for a broken family with poor parents. But there are some aspects from scripture that help. If you are a mother or father who has felt your parenting has brought hurt to your children, let your new desire and direction for your family be to first, love God and second, love your neighbor. This is a reflection of the great commandment shared by Christ in Matthew

22:37-40. As a parent or child, you may be consumed by the plethora of decisions and rules that may accompany a difficult family. All of them ought to hang on these two commands. They will not solve the details, but more importantly, these commands will set the broader long-term direction. Here might be some great questions to ask yourself to break the pattern of brokenness with your children:

1. Are you modeling loving the Lord with all your heart, soul, mind, and strength and loving your neighbor as yourself to your children?

   ____

   ____

   ____

2. Are you seeking to live out the spirit of Joshua's desire: "As for me and my household, we will serve the Lord"?

   ____

   ____

   ____

3. Do you have a regular habit of lovingly disciplining and correcting your children of their wrongdoing, or do you tend to lash out in frustration and anger?

   ____

   ____

   ____

4. Do your children see you primarily loving them, or do they see you as a parent of high expectations, order, and discipline/judgment?

   ____

   ____

   ____

You might be a child who comes from parents who have hurt you. This could be a variety of parent issues from narcissism, neglect, or abuse toward their children. You may have some influence with your parents or none. Again, there are no quick and easy solutions to the brokenness potentially existing with your parents, but here are some reflection questions to help move your household in a direction of healing:

1. Amidst the hurt that you've felt from your parents, are there areas in your life you can thank or encourage your parents for some things they did right?

   ____

   ____

   ____

2. Is there emotional, physical, or sexual abuse that needs to be addressed with a peer or licensed counselor?

   ____

   ____

   ____

3. How can you fulfill the command to "honor your father and mother" while respectfully disagreeing with your parent's past actions or lifestyle?

   ____

   ____

   ____

4. Have you forgiven your parents? (This may be a difficult and long process, and it may not seem fair. As a loving reminder, it wasn't fair when Jesus forgave our sins, but He did and asks us in turn to forgive others.)

   ____

   ____

   ____

Day 4

The Modern Family: Immediate Brokenness

Read: Colossians 3:12-13, 1 Peter 5:7, Revelation 21:1-7, Psalm 34:18, Ephesians 4:31-32, 1 Peter 4:8

We all know people who come from untraditional families. Whether there was divorce, absent fathers, or parents who were never married, our culture has shifted away from the traditional family unit. As western society has become more postmodern and hyper-individualistic, families have suffered in correlation. Here are some staggering statistics:

- Half of all children today will see the breakup of their parent's marriage (CDC), compared to just 8% of children in 1960 (Pew Research Center)
- 21% of children today are being raised without their fathers (Census Bureau)
- 70% of prison inmates incarcerated for long-term sentences grew up in a broken home (U.S. Department of Justice)
- 32% of children are living with an unmarried parent, compared to 13% in 1968 (Pew Research Center)

The residual effects are just as eye-opening:

- Children from divorced parents are more likely to experience behavioral issues between the ages of 7-14 (Marripedia)
- Children from divorce are twice as likely to commit suicide (Science Daily)
- Children from divorce are 5 times more likely to end up in poverty (MDRC)

- Children from divorce are more inclined to premarital sex, cohabitation, and divorce (Focus on the Family)
- Children of divorce are more likely to develop psychological problems when compared to children who lose a parent to death (Demographic Research)

That last statistic was underlined to show the devastating impact divorce can have on a child. I mentioned this earlier, but there are varying degrees of broken home situations. Divorce, separation, and missing parents are situations tending to draw out greater residual effects than other broken family circumstances.

One thing I've discovered over the years is this specific topic doesn't get addressed often. Children from broken or untraditional families either don't want to talk about some of the issues they struggle with or they perceive their situation as what they've always known: normal.

There are also difficult relationship ties between divorced parents, stepparents, and the children. Because of this, it's often easier to withhold talking about this subject in an effort to maintain a surface-level peace. Emotions such as jealousy, anger, and sadness can be expressed too often or suppressed, causing temptation toward a root of bitterness. Family members can even be prone to take sides with certain relatives causing warring factions to be a norm within households.

Conversely, those who were blessed to come from a more traditional single-family unit have not experienced the daily grind of a broken home and might subconsciously expect those who did come from a broken family to just "function normally" into teenage and adult years.

Modern family issues are hard to find in scripture as ancient biblical culture functioned differently, but you don't have to look hard to find examples of brokenness and untraditional households existing in the Old and New Testaments. This is exemplified from kings and patriarchs who took on several wives and concubines with the corresponding brokenness to issues of half-siblings and step-relatives. Sin hasn't just corrupted the modern family, it has left families broken for centuries.

Hope. Rather than looking at the countless examples of extreme broken families within scripture, I wanted to shed light on a family many wouldn't label as untraditional.

Did you know that Jesus did not live in a typical family? His advent and birth story are certainly extraordinary. However, when He entered this world, since He was conceived by the Holy Spirit, Joseph was not His father in the traditional sense.

In fact, Jesus' parents weren't even married when Mary was pregnant. Think of the issues this caused in ancient culture. Many accused Mary of being unfaithful, Joseph had every right to leave her, and Jesus might be labeled as an illegitimate child. In fact, an angel had to appear to Joseph to convince him to not leave Mary, but rather take her home as his wife (Matthew 1:19-21).

Not only was Jesus a part of an untraditional family, but He had a stepdad and half-siblings and/or step-siblings. Some traditions even assert Joseph may have died prematurely before Jesus' crucifixion at 33 years of age. Further, the book of Matthew records the royal lineage of Jesus, which was full of brokenness. Abraham was a liar and coward for hiding behind his wife for protection, Judah convince his brothers to sell his brother Joseph into slavery, Rahab had been a Canaanite prostitute, David committed adultery and murder, Solomon was promiscuous, Ahaz engaged in pagan worship and even burned his sons as an offering to pagan gods. Jesus' family was untraditional and had a lineage full of brokenness.

For years, I had never applied the title of broken to Jesus, especially to His immediate family. I subconsciously assumed Jesus came from a standard family and couldn't sympathize with my brokenness. Perhaps He was put in such a position to be able to relate to those from untraditional families. The apostle Paul shared this about Jesus in Hebrews 4:15:

> *For we do not have a high priest who is unable to sympathize with our weaknesses, but we have one who has been tempted in every way, just as we are – yet was without sin.*

Our High Priest, Savior, and Lord is not a God who is far removed from our brokenness, but who entered into it and endured it without sin.

You might be thinking there are many ways Jesus didn't experience different aspects and details of your broken family, and that might be true, but overall, He lived the untraditional family life.

One aspect we can learn from His situation is that He openly accepted the fathership of Joseph. For those who have stepparents, this can be challenging, especially if you gain a stepparent later in life. On the flip side, think of the role a new stepparent is entering into. They know they must earn trust and respect, possibly realizing they may never ascend to the level of a parent in a child's eyes. I've known well-meaning people who don't acknowledge their step relatives as such, but simply introduce them as, "this is my mom's husband" or, "these are my wife's kids."

I think one of the best things we can learn from the example of Jesus is to embrace family as He does, regardless of how involved they are in your life. This doesn't mean overlooking wrongs or giving into abuse if that's your situation. But what it means is we ought to welcome those who are part of our untraditional family.

This can be very challenging, believe me. As someone who came from divorced parents, then welcomed in stepparents, then went through the unexpected death of a mother in high school, then welcomed in my stepdad's new wife, I realize the challenges that changing untraditional family dynamics and personalities can bring.

Despite the details of brokenness that might plague you daily, I do know this: love can cover over a multitude of sins (1 Peter 4:8). The best thing that you might be able to do is love your stepdad, stepmom, mom's boyfriend, or stepsister, which has the power to overshadow petty disagreements and differences. It may not seem fair to do so, but Jesus who endured the cross for us because He loves us, asks us to also love others.

Next steps. Here are some questions for reflection for those <u>from traditional families</u>:

1. Who are the peers around you who came from a broken household?

____

____

____

2. What are some things you learned or never thought of when you compare your story to those who went through a broken or untraditional family?

____

____

____

3. How can you safely enter into their brokenness and engage them in their story?

____

____

____

4. What are ways you can love those from broken families?

____

____

____

Questions for those <u>from a broken or untraditional family</u>:

1. Have you sat in reflection of the impact your broken family has had on you?

____

____

____

2. Have you embraced the reality of the brokenness of your past and how it will have residual effects on your future?

3. How has your broken family affected your relationships with peers, authority figures, or God?

4. Is there bitterness and envy that has grown in your heart because of your broken family?

5. Do you have safe people to talk to and process through some of the hurt, pain, or effects of an untraditional or broken family?

6. What hope can you gain from God's word as you process through your broken past?

7. What are some ways that you can embrace and love on members of your broken family who are hard to accept or love?

Day 5

No Family: The Broken View of Singleness

Read: 1 Corinthians 7, Matthew 19:1-12

Singleness: the word usually evoking a variety of emotions, from the pre-teen to senior citizen. It's viewed in a wide variety of lenses from a blessing to "Hell on earth." I've been in campus ministry for 13 years, and of all the dreams and passions I've had for shepherding large movements of students, being an expert on singleness was a topic I was never passionate about. I actively avoided it until I realized I was the oldest staff person in our multiple state region who had never married. As students and others wanted to hear more from my experience as a single guy, I knew I needed to embrace my identity in Christ as a single man for the sake of my growth and others.

Singleness is perceived negatively from a worldly standpoint and perhaps more negatively from within the church. From a cultural viewpoint, there seems to be more of an acceptance of singleness as long as you are in a relationship of some sort, whether it's a non-committal relationship, friends with benefits, or just casual promiscuity.

Despite the expectations from culture, however, I've actually felt more pressure from those within the church. I've been asked why I'm still single, and people have assumed I'm lazy and non-committal. Marriage is rightfully and wrongfully equated as a sign of growth and maturity within the church. There are even movements within the church that insinuate that pursuing marriage is an obligation, even if this premise has loose support from scripture.

While nobody would ever say it to me directly, I know I've been overlooked for various opportunities and positions within ministry because of the perception of immaturity or even sinfulness that singleness carries in the church. You may be single for a variety of reasons, and chances are you've never viewed it as a calling similar to marriage.

Hope. How did the church arrive to the era where singles have been similar to second-class citizens? Well, a lot of this perception comes out of the Protestant Reformation. Prior to the Reformation, singleness was actually viewed as a higher calling than marriage in the church. Consider the position of priests, nuns, and monks who took vows of celibacy to serve Christ in the church.

While the Protestant Reformation brought much needed reforms to the church, one of the unintended consequences was a strong reaction toward the Catholic church's stances on many issues that weren't necessarily right or wrong, good or bad issues. One of these was the topic of marriage. From that time period and forward, marriage started to become a higher calling in western civilization. In fact, all the major Protestant reformers (Luther, Zwingli, and Calvin) ended up marrying which was unheard of in church leadership at the time.

This has greatly influenced our modern evangelical churches today. Think of the pastoral staff at your churches. How many of them are single? And if they are single, how many of them have leadership positions over other married staff?

Let me flip this issue. Have you ever thought of singleness as a blessing or gift? You may have perceived it as a curse or just this "cross God is calling you to bear." I've seen people fear singleness to the point of getting married in haste instead of properly waiting. Have you ever realized the two greatest figures in the New Testament, Jesus and Paul, were both single? In fact, Paul encourages others to be single as he is in 1 Corinthians 7:6-7:

> *I say this as a concession, not as a command. I wish that all of you were as I am (single). But each of you has your own gift from God; one has this gift, another has that.*

Throughout the entire chapter, Paul doesn't say marriage or singleness is better than one or the other, but Paul does warn those who are married will have many troubles in life and he wants to spare some from this (1 Corinthians 7:26-28). Jesus also spoke about this issue in Matthew 19:12:

> *"For there are eunuchs who were born that way, and there are eunuchs who have been made eunuchs by others – and there are those who choose to live like eunuchs for the sake of the kingdom of heaven. The one who can accept this should accept it."*

Jesus acknowledges there are eunuchs (those who were castrated or who were devoted to be single) for the sake of the kingdom of God. He even says in Matthew 22:30:

> *"At the resurrection people will neither marry nor be given in marriage."*

As you think about eternity, have you considered marriage as we know it will not even be an institution in heaven? This is certainly a fact you will not hear recited at a wedding!

You may be wondering how singleness is a gift. Well first, you get to bear witness to the sufficiency and fullness of Jesus through your celibacy. You are not giving your body away or hooking up with others because you are married to Jesus, He is sufficient for you and you can be a witness of how Christ is more satisfying than anything this world can offer.

Second, you bear witness to the reality of the resurrection in a unique way. God gives us a unique perspective on the shortness and brevity of life. We live in the reality that Jesus is alive and we will live with Him forever and complete as one member of the vast family of God. We get to display that on earth.

Third, you can fully serve the kingdom of God in ways that marrieds cannot. Through my singleness, I have the unique ability to connect with those I shepherd and have more flexibility to do ministry. I have been on mission to almost every continent to share the gospel and incidentally, see the world! Most married staff and families don't have such unique opportunities as singles serving God's kingdom.

Next steps. If you are single, here are some practical steps to living out your singleness as God intended

1. Be intentional about your status and commit

   There is a difference between how the world lives out singleness and how we ought to live it out in the church. Our culture has a lot of singles who have no intention of committing in relationships, yet want all the benefits that come with the territory. It is popular to be promiscuous, date extensively, and leave things nebulous. This lifestyle has sadly infiltrated the church. Scripture is clear: if you are single, you are to flee from sexual immorality.

Also, just because you are intentional about singleness now, it doesn't mean you need to be single the rest of your life. There are two options within the church for singles. You are either a vowed single or a dedicated single. The vowed single is a person who has committed their lives to being single for the sake of the kingdom of God (more popular in the Orthodox or Catholic traditions). Conversely, the dedicated single is a person who is committed to practicing celibacy as part of their commitment to Christ until they are married.

2. While you are single, live a healthy fulfilled life NOW

   Don't make the mistake of thinking you need to wait until you're married in order to live a fulfilled life in Christ. You will need to build into your daily routine rhythms and boundaries for proper self-care. Often times singles are asked to take on more in ministry because they "have more free time." You may need to fight for yourself.

   Author Parker Palmer says, "I have become clear about at least one thing; self-care is never a selfish act—it is simply good stewardship of the one gift I have, the gift I was put on earth to offer to others."

   You are the limited resource, and in order to steward that, it is vital to discern the kinds of people, places, and activities that bring you joy, restoration, delight, and replenishing so you can be effective in God's kingdom.

Community for singles is vital. I would argue your community is <u>just as important to you as a spouse is to a married couple</u>. This may sound extreme, but it is true. Community for a single person is more difficult to cultivate than a married person. It is way more difficult in busy seasons to cultivate proper community for a single because it isn't naturally built into their living environment like it is for a married person.

Jesus surrounded Himself with close confidants, therefore we need to invest in a few healthy relationships with those we can share with, pray with, cry with, and take joy with.

Whether you are single and enjoy it or yearn to be in a relationship, remember Jesus' promise for eternity in Matthew 19:29-30:

> *"And everyone who has left houses or brothers or sisters or father or mother or wife or children or fields for my sake will receive a hundred times as much and will inherit eternal life. But many who are first will be last, and many who are last will be first."*

Here are some helpful reflection questions to journal on:

1. When you think about your state of marriage or singleness, what thoughts/emotions come to mind?

   ____

   ____

   ____

2. If you are single and don't desire to be, have you been viewing intimate relationships as an idol? Have you thought of singleness as a gift?

____

____

____

3. What have you learned from reading about Jesus' words and Paul's words on marriage and singleness?

____

____

____

4. In what ways can you cultivate your gift of singleness as part of God's kingdom?

____

____

____

5. Are you being intentional about singleness? Are you pursuing healthy community?

____

____

____

6. Are you living singleness like the world or are you being biblically intentional about your sexual morality in the midst of singleness?

____

____

____

7. If you are married, in what way can you be an encouragement to someone in their singleness?

____

____

____

Day 6

The Blended Family: The Brokenness of Loyalties

Read: Matthew 10:34-39, Exodus 20:12, Ephesians 6:1-4, 1 Corinthians 7:12-14

If you are reading this and are a believer, it would be so great if all of your close relatives were believers as well. Often times this might not be the case. There are times when a person becomes a follower of Jesus later in life, which means there may be several relatives who are not believers, including a spouse. When you are talking about a broken family, especially with step and half-relatives, there is a high likelihood there is a blending of believers and non-believers. I have a family comprised of non-believers, nominal Christians, and regenerate believers. This creates expected tension, as there are family members pursuing God's kingdom and some who are pursuing other kingdoms.

Hope. Working in college ministry, I see so many families where this is the case. Perhaps a student came to know Christ on their own and have siblings or parents who aren't believers. I've also known several marriages where one spouse becomes a Christ follower and the other does not. Depending on the cultural background, the residual effects of having believers and non-believers in a family could be a minor or major issue. Perhaps this is what Jesus meant when He said in Matthew 10:34-39:

> *"Do not suppose that I have come to bring peace to the earth. I did not come to bring peace, but a sword. For I have come to turn*

> *'a man against his father,*
> *a daughter against her mother,*
> *a daughter-in-law against her mother-in-law—a man's enemies will be the members of his own household.'*
>
> *Anyone who loves their father or mother more than me is not worthy of me; anyone who loves their son or daughter more than me is not worthy of me. Whoever does not take up their cross and follow me is not worthy of me. Whoever finds their life will lose it, and whoever loses their life for my sake will find it."*

This sounds harsh and unrealistic when you apply it to a blended family of Christians and non-Christians, but could this be the reality? While there is a bonded sense of love and unity, at the core of a believer and non-believer there are vastly different loyalties at heart. One has died to self and is serving a new and righteous King Jesus with His kingdom at heart. The other has not trusted Christ with their life and is serving another kingdom consisting of themselves or a blended version of themselves and worldly ideals. The reality of your family might be a sense of physical and emotional peace, yet vastly different kingdoms warring over what to worship, where to give your time, how to spend money, what is valued, and so much more. Eventually, the loyalties to different kingdoms will surface in how a family functions.

If you are a child who has come to know Jesus in a family consisting of those who do not yet know Christ, here are some ways to live out Christ's kingdom in your own home.

1. Honor Christ first and above all else
2. Love and honor your parents as long as they don't encourage you to abandon Jesus
3. Seek to bring joy to your parents and siblings through small acts of service
4. Prepare for trials and opposition from family members, knowing they will come
5. Be wise in how you interact with family members
6. Pray often for your parents and siblings
7. Give respect to parents instead of resorting to word battles and arguing. This can give great credibility to your words and actions in the future.
8. Trust God has your situation in control and has a plan

If you are looking for direction as a married person with an unbelieving spouse, you may think that the best way to honor God is by separating. The Apostle Paul encourages the exact opposite mentality in 1 Corinthians 7:12-14:

> *To the rest I say this (I, not the Lord): If any brother has a wife who is not a believer and she is willing to live with him, he must not divorce her. And if a woman has a husband who is not a believer and he is willing to live with her, she must not divorce him. For the unbelieving husband has been sanctified through his wife, and the unbelieving wife has been sanctified through her believing husband. Otherwise your children would be unclean, but as it is, they are holy.*

Sanctified here can also be translated into holy. This is not referring to a spiritual or personal holiness, but a family or matrimonial holiness. By staying married to your non-believing spouse, you have the opportunity to bring God's blessing and provision to your household. A spouse doesn't automatically become a Christ follower because their spouse believes. It is a decision each person needs to individually make. However, there is supernatural fruit of the Spirit at work through the believing spouse in that household which brings love, joy, peace, patience, kindness, goodness, faithfulness, gentleness, and self-control to an unbelieving spouse and children. Through this matrimonial holiness brought by a believing spouse, who knows the relatives of your household who may one day also come to know Jesus?

Next steps. If you are from a blended family of believers and non-believers, here are some reflection questions to help you consider the reality and hope of your situation:

For children with unbelieving parents and siblings:

1. What are ways you can thank, honor, and bless your parents or siblings?

   ____

   ____

   ____

2. Have you had the opportunity to share what Jesus has done in your life?

   ____

   ____

   ____

3. Do you have believing friends and respected Christian leaders you could confide in about how to approach your blended family?

   ____

   ____

   ____

4. Are there other believers in your family you could confide in about how to love your non-believing family members?

____

____

____

5. Have you invited family members to church, bible study, or other Christian gatherings?

____

____

____

6. How can you adjust your rhetoric and language toward your parents or siblings so your words for Christ might gain credibility from their perspective?

____

____

____

For those married to an unbelieving spouse:

1. Have you had conversations about the influence for Christ you might have on your children?

____

____

____

2. What are ways you can share about how Jesus has changed your life?

____

____

____

3. Do you have other Christians through a small group or church you can confide in about how to love your spouse as a believer?

____

____

____

4. Have you invited your spouse to social events or gatherings of other Christians?

____

____

____

5. Have you had the hard conversations about how you spend your time and money that is honoring to God?

____

____

____

6. Are there aspects of your behavior you need to adjust in order to be a better witness for Christ to your spouse?

____

____

____

Day 7

Goodbye Brother: The Brokenness of Separation

Read: Genesis 21:1-21, Genesis 32-33

I watched a movie recently with a mix of comedy and slow burn drama. The family had gathered for the funeral of a recently deceased father. There were some instigators to the family drama, but every relative had a contributing factor to the divisiveness. The end of the movie had profound sadness as three sisters parted ways with each other and their mother on terrible terms with the intention of never seeing each other again.

I reasoned this was just Hollywood sensationalism devoid of reality. However, as I turned the mirror back on my own family, I realize there are situations among extended relatives where some have chosen to never speak to or about another relative. I wrote earlier of the reality as divisions grow, there are some people who willingly settle to cut ties with relatives all-together. There could be legitimate and honorable reasons for doing this in cases of abuse or physical harm, but for the vast majority of those I've witnessed, it is for petty and prideful reasons.

Perhaps you are in a situation where you've dug yourself so deep with other relatives, a reunion would be utterly painful. Or, you are in a situation where others have cut ties with you for life choices, disagreements, or even your decision to follow Jesus. Maybe you've made an honorable choice to cut ties with relatives based on a history of abuse and toxicity, yet you desire some sort of healthy reconciliation.

Hope. There are many instances in Scripture of people who have severed ties with each other. One of the more famous examples is the division within Abraham's family. Abraham had two sons, Ishmael, whose mother was Hagar, and Isaac, whose mother was Sarah. Genesis 21:8-14 elaborates on the separation:

> *The child grew and was weaned, and on the day Isaac was weaned Abraham held a great feast. But Sarah saw that the son whom Hagar the Egyptian had borne to Abraham was mocking, and she said to Abraham, "Get rid of that slave woman and her son, for that woman's son will never share in the inheritance with my son Isaac."*
>
> *The matter distressed Abraham greatly because it concerned his son. But God said to him, "Do not be so distressed about the boy and your slave woman. Listen to whatever Sarah tells you, because it is through Isaac that your offspring will be reckoned. I will make the son of the slave into a nation also, because he is your offspring."*
>
> *Early the next morning Abraham took some food and a skin of water and gave them to Hagar. He set them on her shoulders and then sent her off with the boy. She went on her way and wandered in the Desert of Beersheba.*

God had promised Abraham and Sarah a son, but in their haste, Abraham agreed with Sarah to bear a son through a servant, Hagar. Years later, Sarah became pregnant and gave birth to Isaac, yet she could not stand the presence and competition within the family, so she callously demanded they leave, which Abraham reluctantly honored.

Now, the separation of these siblings has rich symbolism in the New Testament when comparing the Law versus the Promise of God. However, the symbolism does not address the actual family predicament of Abraham's relatives who severed ties with each other. Despite their separation, God provided for both Isaac and Ishmael.

Many believe the modern divisions between Jews and Arabs stem all the way back to this instance of separation between Isaac and Ishmael. In fact, when you think of modern struggles between people groups across the world, the divisions make sense when you trace them back to an era or historical event taking place generations ago. Yet the animosity thrives.

Let reconciliation be your guide when approaching relatives who have parted ways. There may be setbacks and harsh rhetoric along the way, but unless there is one party willing to move toward reconciliation, division will continue, potentially affecting subsequent generations.

Thankfully with Isaac and Ishmael, the story doesn't end. We don't know about the future relationship of Isaac and Ishmael, but we know they came together at Abraham's funeral to bury him together in Genesis 25:9, indicating some sort of familial harmony.

However, the same situation also occurs with Isaac and his sons, Jacob and Esau. After Jacob tricked Isaac into giving him Esau's firstborn blessing, the two brothers separate and Jacob feared Esau. Years later, they meet and Jacob fears the worst with this reunion. Yet Esau, the original offended party, embraces his brother as Genesis 33:1-5 records:

Jacob looked up and there was Esau, coming with his four hundred men; so he divided the children among Leah, Rachel and the two female servants. He put the female servants and their children in front, Leah and her children next, and Rachel and Joseph in the rear. [3] *He himself went on ahead and bowed down to the ground seven times as he approached his brother.*

But Esau ran to meet Jacob and embraced him; he threw his arms around his neck and kissed him. And they wept. Then Esau looked up and saw the women and children. "Who are these with you?" he asked.

Jacob answered, "They are the children God has graciously given your servant."

Jacob and Esau both humbly embraced each other. Esau initiated to embrace Jacob, while Jacob referred to himself as a servant of Esau.

Notice what didn't happen here: There was not an exchange of words or mistakes from the past. While it may be healthy to address those down the road of reconciliation, this moment was all about reunion. Both recognized the alienation between each other and perhaps they saw the drastic effects from the poor example of their father Isaac and uncle Ishmael and instead desired for their families to reconcile with each other.

Reconciliation between two parties cannot happen unless one party humbly initiates. We cannot control how others may respond, but that doesn't mean we stop pursuing. You may think it's not fair to pursue a relative who has left, but think about what God did to reconcile you to Himself. He pursued us even in our rebellion against Him until you were reconciled to Him. God seeks the same reconciliation between you and broken relationships with others, however long and difficult.

Next steps. Here are some reflection questions when considering relatives who have separated.

For those who have had relatives break relationship over disputable or drama related issues:

1. What steps are you taking to move toward a reconciled relationship versus adding to the division?

   ____

   ____

   ____

2. Have you sought the advice of wise godly counsel outside of your family? (Remember, the intent is to seek advice on reconciliation, not to gossip about division)

   ____

   ____

   ____

3. Can you overlook the offense that caused the disruption in a relationship for the sake of moving toward each other?

   ____

   ____

   ____

4. Many wise counselors would say indifference, not hate, is the opposite of love. Are you being indifferent toward a broken family tie?

   ____

   ____

   ____

5. Do you have children who might be missing out on important family relationships because of irreconcilable differences?

    ____

    ____

    ____

6. Is this relationship separation due to a difference in religion? As a believer, have you initiated this separation to take an easy path of growing in your faith while avoiding loving difficult relatives?

    ____

    ____

    ____

For those who have had serious offenses that have warranted an honorable separation from a family member (issues of considerable abuse):

1. Have you sought counseling services to address the offense against you?

    ____

    ____

    ____

2. Have you named the offense a family member has perpetrated toward you? (Emotional abuse, improper boundaries, sexual abuse, physical abuse, etc.)

    ____

    ____

    ____

3. What could create a safe situation and cause you to move toward this broken relationship?

    ____

    ____

    ____

4. Are you ignoring signs indicating your relative may sincerely desire to reconcile with you?

____

____

____

5. Does the other person know the extent of their offense or could the hurt you experienced be brought safely in conversation?

____

____

____

6. Is this separation due to a shunning because of your faith in Christ and you are trying to protect yourself from harm or danger? Are there safe ways you can express the love of Christ toward these relatives?

____

____

____

7. Are you a third party in the midst of relatives who have cut ties with each other and are there ways you could delicately push toward reconciliation?

____

____

____

Day 8

Unexpected Loss: The Brokenness of Death

Read: Job 1-2, Luke 13:1-5, 2 Corinthians 1:1-11

In high school, I yearned for popularity. I had only lived in Ohio for a few years after moving from Wisconsin. I was slowly getting to know more and more people and was starting to be recognized.

One day, I was called out of class in uncharacteristic fashion to come down to the main office. When I arrived, the first person I saw was my sister, and I realized the issue was family related, not academic. The superintendent told us our mom had suffered a brain aneurysm and had been helicoptered to a hospital in Columbus.

When we arrived, our worst fears were realized in that my mom had passed away. We were devastated. I was shocked and confused. Years later, I realized in an ironic twist, I was instantly known throughout the whole school, but in a tragic way I never wanted.

At the time, I thought unexpected deaths only happened to other families. For those reading this who have gone through the unexpected loss of a close relative, you know the shock and pain all too well. Instantly, the small struggles of life pale in comparison to the loss you've endured.

The topic of life, death, purpose, eternity can become the center of one's thoughts. Some people question God's goodness, others become bitter or even angry at God and people around them. Some ignore the grieving process and act like nothing even happened. Others wear immense grief on their shoulders without seeking proper healing and can overburden others. After experiencing years of ministry, I have seen all of these responses. I will even readily admit I have made mistakes in my own grieving process. There are no clear answers on how to navigate unexpected loss.

Hope. Suffering from loss can bring much confusion as you attempt to connect faith and suffering. The book of Job highlights a righteous man who endured the loss of his wealth, health, and most of his family due to natural disasters and raiding warriors. Before going through suffering, Job is described as upright and blameless (Job 1:1). This raises the age-old question, "Why do bad things happen to good people?"

The remainder of Job highlights a lengthy discourse between Job and his friends who assume God sent suffering on Job because of his sin. In fact, a very simplistic view of suffering which has endured through the centuries is those who suffer are more sinful while those who are blessed and prosper are more righteous. Our culture still believes the notion "If I lead a good life, God will reward and bless me."

Instead of comforting Job during his grieving process, his friends give him poor advice and are ultimately rebuked by God in the end. God then blessed Job beyond what he even had before tragedy came. It seems like in this specific situation, God put Job through a testing period to show his faith was genuine even amidst hardship.

We look at stories of suffering in scripture and can assume the reason we are going through suffering is for the exact same reason. This could be true, however, there are many different reasons God might have us go through suffering. Here are 5 reasons that suffering might happen:

1. **Suffering as a form of discipline for your sin**. This can be the easiest to identify. For example, if you are promiscuous and contract an STD, this is a natural consequence and suffering due to sin.
2. **Suffering may enable us to identify with those who go through similar struggles.** In 2 Corinthians 1, Paul says a person who has suffered through a specific hardship might be better equipped to connect with those who are enduring the same suffering. I feel more confident and resourceful when coming alongside those who have gone through the death of a parent.
3. **Suffering helps us draw closer to God.** Suffering can help us flee the temporal pleasures of the world to help remind us who is in control and what is eternally significant. If you come alongside a devout believer who has gone through suffering, there will probably be a story of wrestling with God and emerging closer to Him.
4. **Suffering reminds us this world is not our home.** This may be the greatest lesson I learned through my tragedy. My eyes were opened to the reality of my temporary home on earth compared to eternity with Christ. This may also be why Jesus spends so much time talking about the blessed state of the poor compared to the wealthy. The poor have a greater and clearer vision of hope in Christ because there is very little in this world they are holding on to for hope and satisfaction.
5. **Suffering might just be a result of living your faith in a broken world.** Sometimes, we don't know the full reason why we suffer, or it may be a subtle mix of several of the reasons listed above. You aren't entitled

to know the full picture or reasoning. Faith in God means just that: trusting in Him despite not knowing the full picture or all the details of His will.

The process of grieving and discovering God's purpose in your suffering won't be instantaneous like downloading an app. The process may take weeks, months, or even years.

It has been 23 years since my mom's death and I still express emotion and don't fully know the reason as to why God took her. However, there are a few things I've learned. One, my life's purpose has never been the same, but in a good way. I discovered the brevity of life in comparison to God and eternity and submitted my life to Jesus not only as Savior, but also as King over my life.

Two, I have been able to come alongside many students and friends who have gone through similar tragedies. I might not have many answers, but I have the comfort of relating to their experience.

Three, I won't need vision as to the importance of sharing my faith as I deeply recognize our time here is limited. There are lost people that need to hear the good news of Jesus.

Lastly, my priorities in this world have been shifted from pursuing the "American Dream" and a lucrative life to one centered on God's Kingdom and His purposes.

As a final encouragement, please know grieving is a healthy and important process when you've lost a loved one. Death was not supposed to be part of creation until the Fall, which is why we respond in mourning.

In our western triumphal culture, it can be tempting to put a positive spin or provide all the answers in the midst of suffering. I have seen too many people go through tragedy and reenter life like nothing happened. This is very unhealthy and may cause you to become desensitized to your emotions when future hardship hits. I struggled in this area, and saw suppressed emotions surface years later.

On the flip side, I have also seen those who over-grieve by putting too much emotional baggage on others and wearing their suffering on their shoulders for all to constantly see. If you are struggling with the grieving process or feel like you didn't properly go through that process, you may want to consider grief counseling. Often times churches offer such services for those going through the loss of loved ones.

Lastly, have grace on yourself through the grieving process. Since death is an unnatural consequence of the original Fall, there is no rulebook on grieving. Most look back at their grieving experiences and recognize mistakes made along the way. Don't dwell on them; rather, take the things you learned to comfort those who will go through the same type of suffering.

Next steps. Here are some reflection questions to help you in your grieving process:

1. How long ago did your tragic loss occur and what did the process look like for grieving?

   ____

   ____

   ____

2. Are there close friends or relatives you feel safe confiding in about the emotions and changes you've gone through?

____

3. What have you learned through your suffering? (It's ok to not know the answer to this for many years)

4. As you assess your grieving process, did you have a proper time of grieving? Did you over-grieve?

5. Are there others in your life who have gone through similar tragedies who you could reach out to be a comfort or encouragement to?

6. Do you feel comfortable opening up and talking about your loss with friends or in small groups?

7. In your grieving, have you sought counsel and insight from others who have experienced similar loss?

8. How has your life changed since your loss? How have you approached suffering and faith?

Day 9

The American Dream: The Brokenness of Wealth

Read: Mark 10:17-31, Matthew 6:24

The contrast of lifestyles I lived couldn't be more real growing up. When I was in second grade, I remember the tiny house my mom, sister, and I lived in. It had two bedrooms and one bathroom with a makeshift room downstairs. Mom was finishing her college degree at the time and money was so tight, we even qualified for free lunch at school.

Fast forward seven years – not only did my mom have a good career, but she remarried to an engineer. We had moved to a more affluent neighborhood in a very large house with a gorgeous backyard on the edge of a hill. It even had a built-in hot tub on the back deck. Regular trips to the country club were a norm as our family now knew doctors, lawyers, and judges. As my childhood progressed, I had tasted the "American Dream."

In high school, I knew I wanted this "American Dream" when I grew up. So, I needed to get into a good major at a prestigious university, which I set out to do and succeeded. I still wanted to pursue my faith, but also wanted to subtly work hard toward a lavish lifestyle.

Fast forward to my mid-20's. Through a variety of circumstances, I lost the career I worked so hard for and found myself joining campus ministry full-time. This shocking transition even led a close relative to sit me down and ask why I would waste my engineering degree.

Through the process, I felt the weight of disappointment and confusion from some friends and family. I had realized through a long and painstaking process that I could serve God as my master or I could serve money, but I could not serve both.

Hope. This may seem like a category that confuses most as it doesn't seem to be related to brokenness. As a friendly reminder, this devotional seeks to address brokenness within families as God sees it, not as culture sees brokenness.

Many of you might have grown up in a prestigious family with a nice home, family, and influence. You might not even realize how the "American Dream" has captivated your family. You may not view the "Dream" as "all that bad." You may not even realize how wealthy your family is or the opportunities it provided.

One thing I learned over the years is the subtle deception of wealth to provide satisfaction, especially if having money was normal growing up. I happen to have wealthy relatives who have boldly declared they aren't rich.

Wealth has become a normal part of our culture. Globally however, according to sportofmoney.com, 31% of global wealth is in the United States and the average American's salary is 25 times greater than the average global salary. Regardless of how you may compare, chances are extremely high you are wealthy in the eyes of the world. The deception of wealth that we face seems to rarely satisfy and always recognizes there is someone wealthier. Simultaneously, the temptation is there are always more opportunities to gain more wealth.

This is why biblical verses where Jesus addresses money are so cringeworthy to us. We even try to justify our wealth by reinterpreting or providing a false application to them. Jesus' words should hit home and change our lifestyle and focus. On one occasion, a wealthy man approaches Jesus and asks what he must do to inherit eternal life. After some discussion, Jesus responds by saying in Mark 10:21-22:

> *Jesus looked at him and loved him. "One thing you lack," he said. "Go, sell everything you have and give to the poor, and you will have treasure in heaven. Then come, follow me."*
>
> *At this the man's face fell. He went away sad, because he had great wealth.*

The rich man's response seems so sad. Rather than following the God of the universe, he turns away and continues to devote himself to his wealth.

How many of us are doing this without realizing it? How many of us want the best of both worlds: an authentic relationship with Jesus and a lucrative job, large house, or affluent lifestyle? Not only did Jesus continue by saying how hard it is for a rich man to enter the kingdom of God, but elsewhere He says in Matthew 6:24:

> *"No one can serve two masters. Either you will hate the one and love the other, or you will be devoted to the one and despise the other. You cannot serve both God and money.*

I tried for many years to carefully serve God and money, yet it does not work because both masters have different agendas and ideals at heart. This might be an area of brokenness plaguing most families in our culture, including those within the church, and even among ministry staff.

It is vitally important for an honest self-reflection of our heart when it comes to money. It's this very master potentially preventing you and your family from serving God with all your heart, or even being part of His kingdom.

Next steps. Here are some reflection questions for healthy self-assessment on the topic of money within your family:

1. Where do you stand with the two masters of God and money?

   ____
   ____
   ____

2. How much of the "American Dream" have you personally bought into?

   ____
   ____
   ____

3. Why did you choose the career path or major that you did?

   ____
   ____
   ____

4. If you were to lose almost all of your wealth, would Jesus still be enough?

   ____
   ____
   ____

5. Look at the financial transactions you've made in the last few months. Are they reflecting serving God's kingdom or your own desires?

____
____
____

6. What does your giving situation look like? Are you giving at least 10% of your income to the church or other ministries?

____
____
____

7. Do you give begrudgingly or with a cheerful heart?

____
____
____

8. When you give, are any of your dollars going toward missions in the 10/40 window? (*joshuaproject.net* to learn more about the 10/40 window)

____
____
____

9. If you realize you've been serving the "American Dream", what are steps you can take to begin turning that around and serving God's kingdom?

____
____
____

10. What has your love for money prevented you from doing to serve God?

____
____
____

Day 10

Sexual Brokenness: The Price of Deceptive Freedom

Read: 1 Kings 11:1-13

Sex has gone through major cultural shifts in the last half-century that has coincided with family brokenness. Once revered as a sacred boundary of consummation between a man and woman in the covenant of marriage, it's been tarnished by the sexual revolution.

Culture has shifted from recognizing clear boundaries related to the good gift of sex and instead has redefined sexual norms. I don't have to share much evidence as our culture and media is addicted to the topic. Sex outside of marriage is now normal and encouraged, living with a boyfriend or girlfriend before marriage is expected, there are "hook up" apps that make finding random sexual partners simple and fast. Additionally, the LGBTQIA+ movement is a recent and emotionally explosive topic, abortion is labeled as a birth control right, and pornography is a multi-billion-dollar industry. The recent acceptable sexual trend seems to be as long as a person, or people, are of age and consent, any form of sexuality is acceptable.

As sexuality has turned from a God-given covenant to a western individualistic freedom, culture has paid a dear price. Over the last 60 years divorce rates have spiked to around 40-50% of all marriages (motherjones.com), families with parents who were never married has skyrocketed from 7% to 25% (Pew Research Center), the spread of STDs has increased to 20% of the entire population (CDC), and abortion has become a multi-billion-dollar industry (IBIS World). Those are the hard tangibles.

It's less difficult to measure when someone crosses emotional and physical barriers. When a person gives themselves to another sexually, there is a deep emotional and physical bond. More sex leads to becoming desensitized to this bond, which, perhaps is what they want in the short term. If this person ultimately decides to get married, these physical and emotional bonds have become desensitized, presenting a real challenge for intimacy with their spouse. Along with that, there may be several images of other men or women coming to mind when becoming intimate with your spouse due to the overstimulation of past sexual partners and pornographic images. These represent many of the intangible consequences culture tries to ignore or downplay.

Oftentimes, relational strains can be a root cause of a person's sexual brokenness. It's hard to quantify emotional wounds, but there seems to be a strong correlation between how a child bonds with a parent, especially a father. An absent father could mean a sexualized unhealthy attachment to another man.

The Dad Resource Center finds the father-daughter relationship has a huge impact on a girl's sexual development. Those with poor father figures are more likely to engage in risky sexual behavior. In fact, sons and daughters without a father in their home were 33% more likely to have sex before the age of 17.

Additionally, LGBTQIA+ ideation can stem from emotional brokenness in the home between a child and one or both parents. A person can easily try to medicate those emotional voids with sexual fantasies and physical intimacy with one or both genders. So many issues of sexual brokenness can stem from a lack of parental emotional bonding or an abuse of parental emotional bonding from within a broken home.

The greatest offense, however, in sexual brokenness is the rebellion against God's will. We are commanded to flee from sexual immorality (Ephesians 5:3). Not only is sexual activity outside the covenant of a marriage between a man and a woman rebellion against God, but being intimate with the wrong person can steer you away from fellowship with God and others. God does not seek to restrain enjoyment – in fact, He created it. But He wants it to be done in the context of a covenantal relationship with a spouse who is also pursuing God. He seeks boundaries to protect us from ultimate harm done against Him, ourselves, and others.

Hope. You might be reading up to this point and feel the weight of conviction of your sexual history or your support of culture's warped view of sexuality in general. You don't have to look far in scripture to find those who have also abused the gift of sexuality.

One instance was a tragic ending to a story of a man who was considered the wisest in the world. He was king of the most influential kingdom in the world at that time. Dignitaries from across the world traveled to seek his wisdom. This man was the third king of Israel, Solomon. Despite his intention to follow God and the wisdom he was gifted, his promiscuity to many women led to his downfall. 1 Kings 11:4 records:

> *As Solomon grew old, his wives turned his heart after other gods, and his heart was not fully devoted to*

> *the* Lord *his God, as the heart of David his father had been.*

At one point, Solomon had 700 wives and 300 concubines. His sexual desires for many women cost him in his devotion to God. Solomon's father, King David, caused much suffering to the entire nation of Israel by his affair with Bathsheba. Perhaps Solomon unintentionally learned these broken sexual habits from his father.

Next steps. If you are someone who has had a past of sexual brokenness and are overwhelmed by the weight of your sin, there's good news: Jesus died for your guilt and shame. He offers forgiveness to a repentant heart, no matter the trespass. Romans 8:1 assures us:

> *Therefore, there is now no condemnation for those who are in Christ Jesus, because through Christ Jesus the law of the Spirit who gives life has set you free from the law of sin and death.*

A repentant heart is not just someone who is sorry for their sin, but confesses their sin to God and repents (or turns) from their ways. Jesus even said when He saved the woman from stoning as she was caught in adultery in John 8:11:

> *"Then neither do I condemn you," Jesus declared. "Go now and leave your life of sin."*

True repentance and forgiveness come when there is confession (agreeing with God over your sin and wrongdoing) and then turning from your old ways to God.

Here are some helpful reflection questions as you assess your own sexual brokenness, the brokenness of your family, and the sexual brokenness of those who influence you:

1. If you have been sexually active with an unmarried person or several people, what are you doing to repent?

   ____

   ____

   ____

2. You may not be involved sexually with others, but struggle with pornography and masturbation. What are you actively doing to turn from this sin?

   ____

   ____

   ____

3. Are there former sexual partners who you may need to follow up and seek forgiveness from?

   ____

   ____

   ____

4. Have you been involved with others sexually or through pornography? Have you become desensitized to intimacy?

   ____

   ____

   ____

5. What are areas in your life you can change or cut out (social media, night entertainment, the gym, etc.) to prevent sexual arousal or temptation?

   ____

   ____

   ____

6. If you are married and have a family, is there undisclosed promiscuity you need to address with your spouse or family?

____

____

____

7. Are there unhealthy sexual temptations with the same gender or those underage that need to be addressed with others?

____

____

____

8. Is there sexual trauma or abuse from your past you haven't addressed with a counselor?

____

____

____

9. Do you fantasize about others while engaged in intimacy with your spouse?

____

____

____

10. For men, are you acting out physically in regard to sexual temptation with a girlfriend? For women, are you improperly fantasizing far beyond where a relationship currently is with another man?

____

____

____

Day 11

Family Tradition: Blinding Eyes from the Truth

Read: Mark 7:1-13

I will readily admit: I love traditions, especially family ones! Similarly, you may be looking forward to that holiday, camping trip, summer getaway, birthday celebration, or whatever tradition your family holds dear. I cannot wait each year to see extended relatives at holidays and campouts. I look forward to Thanksgiving and Christmas traditions. In fact, I am usually the first person to voice opposition to stopping a time-honored tradition knowing how much joy they have brought in my life.

Traditions, however, can be both a blessing and a curse. The blessings of joy, family, excitement, and community are obvious. The curses of family traditions, however, are more subtle.

Oftentimes, we form traditions around holidays and celebrations and as these traditions grow, we become consumed with details like presents, food dishes, appropriate visiting time, housing arrangements, or even comfort, rather than the purpose of a holiday or celebration itself.

Traditions within faith can also have consequences. A person can get so preoccupied in traditions that the heart of worship can be completely lost. There is a Broadway song that proclaims great pride in the tradition of one's religion. An entire verse of this song highlights how tradition guides everything from eating to sleeping and even how to wear clothes. One verse states: "You may ask, how did this tradition start? I'll tell you – I don't know." How true is this of holiday and faith traditions? Oftentimes many who observe time-honored traditions within a church service or holiday tradition don't even know the purpose behind them. Tradition can provide lip-service to faith, but blind a person to knowing God.

Families today aren't the only people who struggle with the curses of tradition. The most famous adversaries of Jesus, the Pharisees, were stooped in tradition. These were some of the most religious people you could imagine from our perspective. They knew scripture well and some even had it memorized. Everything from their schedule, conversation, and clothing revolved around their devotion to the details of scripture and tradition.

Jesus does the unthinkable and actually calls them out in their unrighteousness. The Pharisees had just accused Jesus' disciples of not washing their hands before eating, which was not a biblical command, but a man-made tradition that the Pharisees held on to along with many other traditions. Jesus responds in Mark 7:8:

> *"You have let go of the commands of God and are holding on to human traditions."*

The Pharisees became so obsessed with their elder's and forefather's traditions they neglected the greater aspects of God's commands. Perhaps this is why Jesus proclaimed harshly in Matthew 23:23-24:

> *"Woe to you, teachers of the law and Pharisees, you hypocrites! You give a tenth of your spices—mint, dill and cumin. But you have neglected the more*

important matters of the law—justice, mercy and faithfulness. You should have practiced the latter, without neglecting the former. You blind guides! You strain out a gnat but swallow a camel."

The sad irony is the Pharisees were so blinded by their traditions, they failed to see the very God they proclaimed in the flesh right in front of them. Can you see how traditions can cause subtle blindness in the greater aspects of worshiping God? Can you see how we can ignore justice, compassion and mercy to others, be faithless toward God, and neglect authentic fellowship with others?

Hope. Perhaps your family needs to re-evaluate spiritual gatherings and celebrations and ask what the purpose of these events are. Instead of focusing so much on gifts, clothes, social gatherings, and decorating, maybe Christmas ought to be about worshiping the first coming of our Savior and King. Instead of social gatherings where the same surface conversations emerge, perhaps there are greater opportunities to engage deeply with others. Instead of a wedding day with many traditional aspects, perhaps there is an emphasis on prayer and a focus on the marriage's ultimate reflection of Christ's consummation with the church. Are there ways that your family can incorporate a discussion or devotional time around a recently attended church sermon or important events in the church calendar? There are many ways a family can keep certain traditions without letting them blind you and others to Christ and deeper fellowship with His body.

This probably won't be easy. While you might be determined to realign your family's focus past mere tradition, this doesn't mean everyone else will have the same vision or desired change. This change might take effect in your life and a few others, but the sad reality is there are people like the Pharisees who will desire to be hardened in their position to continue to focus on tradition rather than more important matters of God's heart. Taking next steps might not be easy and you may even experience resistance, but you may be called to take the hard step of trying to see a shift from mere tradition to an authentic heart of worship.

Next steps. Here are reflection questions to guide your thoughts about traditions within your family and brainstorm ways and opportunities to refocus them on loving God and others:

1. What are some of the greatest traditions you look forward to with your family?

   ____

   ____

   ____

2. Think about your holiday celebrations, how many are traditions that detract from worshiping God and authentic fellowship with others?

   ____

   ____

   ____

3. What are some changes you can make within your family during holiday gatherings that could move you and others toward God?

   ____

   ____

   ____

4. Are you comfortable with taking the easy route and continuing traditions to not create family tension or are you committed to looking past traditions for the sake of worshiping God and going deeper with others?

   ____

   ____

   ____

5. Are you actively involved in the planning process of family gatherings or do you desire to go with the flow and allow others to dictate family norms and traditions?

   ____

   ____

   ____

6. What are some practical steps you are going to take to reorient your life and invite family in on transitioning from tradition to an authentic heart of worship around the following:

Christmas/Easter: ______________________________

Family Celebration: ____________________________

Reflecting on a Church Service or Talk: ______________

Camping Trip: _________________________________

Cabin Trip/Summer Getaway: _____________________

Car Rides: ____________________________________

Family Reunions: _______________________________

Day 12

The Difficult Marriage: The War of Cultural Ideals

Read: 1 Corinthians 12:31-13:13, Ephesians 5:21-33

As a single man who is not married, I feel the least qualified to address the topic of difficult marriages in this devotional. However, despite my relationship status, I have been invited into several marriages to give counsel and even officiate wedding ceremonies. There are certainly godly ideals to impart on the difficult marriage, even from an outside perspective.

Before I go further, I want to address something. Marriage difficulties can come in varying degrees. There are cases with extreme situations in marriages which might warrant a temporary or permanent separation due to safety concerns regarding children or yourself. Situations such as heavy emotional abuse or physical abuse should be addressed with either close peers, a trusted pastor, a licensed counselor, or even law enforcement. If this sounds like you, I highly encourage you to discretely reach out to a trusted friend or a local counselor for next steps.

For those who are struggling in a marriage with lesser degrees of difficulty, perhaps there needs to be a major shift from how you've understood love from a cultural perspective.

A biblical ideal greatly contrasting with western individualism and the sexual revolution is the concept of love being a choice, not just a feeling. Too often, we make rash decisions based on feelings and what will fulfill us now. However, love in the context of a marriage covenant should not be guided by feelings, but a commitment. I don't care how much you are infatuated with your newlywed spouse now and how you could never imagine being apart. There will be a time when you are not feeling the love you once did and you might desire something different. This is where commitment and the choice to love your spouse will differ greatly from the world.

Hope. Scripture is full of hints and examples of different marriages, and we often see a negative glimpse of these marriages. One scripture passage you will hear often at a Christian wedding is from 1 Corinthians 13. In this section of scripture, Paul reminds his readers what true love looks like. He is not just speaking about marriage, but Paul is addressing love in a much broader context. Hear Paul's words on love in 1 Corinthians 13:1-8:

> *If I speak in the tongues of men or of angels, but do not have love, I am only a resounding gong or a clanging cymbal. If I have the gift of prophecy and can fathom all mysteries and all knowledge, and if I have a faith that can move mountains, but do not have love, I am nothing. If I give all I possess to the poor and give over my body to hardship that I may boast, but do not have love, I gain nothing. Love is patient, love is kind. It does not envy, it does not boast, it is not proud. It does not dishonor others, it is not self-seeking, it is not easily angered, it keeps no record of wrongs. Love does not delight in evil but rejoices with the truth. It always protects, always trusts, always hopes, always perseveres. Love never fails.*

Perhaps to help our desensitized understanding of this scripture, it might help to read this passage in a modern context (my translation):

"If I have an incredible prayer life and am eloquent in speaking to others, yet I don't show love, it doesn't matter. If I am well educated and work hard to earn the respect of my peers and elders and even know scripture better than others, but don't have love, its worthless. If I am a generous philanthropist and sacrifice so much to get ahead, yet don't love, I've gained nothing. Instead, love is patient with those who do wrong or disagree with me. Love does not grow jealous of the accomplishments of those around me. It is gentle and caring. It doesn't embellish my own accomplishments and seek the right to be right. It doesn't subtly seek to tear others down or negatively level the playing field. Love does not focus on my wants and needs compared to those around me. Love means I am slow and seldom to anger. It does not have a list of grievances or wrongs to hold over someone. Love doesn't encourage sin and rebellion, but celebrates and takes joy in what is right. Love protects others even if it means a collapse or danger to myself. Love means trust is my lead foot. Love is not pessimistic, but has clear vision of hope and perseveres through difficult trials. Love far surpasses all other worldly goals and ideals."

Sounds a little different when Paul's words are given a modern application, doesn't it? In Ephesians 5, Paul takes this further in addressing husbands and wives with ideals our culture not only doesn't understand, but that some vehemently hate. He encourages wives to submit to their husbands, and in turn, asks husbands to love your wives as Christ loved the church. He uses the concept of marriage to reveal the greater aspect of Christ as the bridegroom being united to the Church, His bride.

Upon first reading this, wives may assume they unfairly have the worse role in a marriage. However, remember what Christ did for the Church. He loved the Church so much, He died to protect and save her. Husbands have the challenging, but loving role, to sacrifice for their wives, even if it means with their career, reputation, social standing, or their life. This is the standard a marriage should strive for: a reflection of the beautiful relationship between Christ and His Church.

Has this been what love looks like toward your spouse? Chances are you have looked at this high bar and recognized you've failed at several aspects of loving your spouse. This is why it is important to put Jesus is at the center of your marriage. Not only does He offer the unconditional love that forgives us of our wrongdoing, but He provides the example of sacrificial love for us. We rely on the Holy Spirit to guide us through the difficult aspects of a marriage with Christ at the center. You will not be perfect at loving your spouse, but prayerfully this is the continual goal that a husband and wife are moving toward: striving to reflect the love between Christ and the Church.

Next steps. Here are questions to assess your marriage:

1. What thoughts come to mind in your marriage when you read 1 Corinthians 13?

   ____

   ____

   ____

2. What thoughts arise when you think of love from 1 Corinthians 13 in the context of loving others?

___

___

___

3. Does your marriage model that of Ephesians 5:21-33?

___

___

___

4. If you know there is a disconnect in your marriage, have you sought wise counsel from peers/mentors or sought counseling together?

___

___

___

5. For husbands, what are you not sacrificing for your marriage and family? Career? Respect? Reputation? Sports? Social life?

___

___

___

6. For wives, in what ways are you not submitting to your husband? Don't let "submit" be defined by our culture, instead understand the biblical definition.

___

___

___

7. For both husbands and wives, what does Ephesians 5:21 (submitting to one another out of reverence for Christ), mean for you and your marriage?

___

___

___

8. Has there been emotional or physical abuse not addressed in your marriage? Is this abuse to the point where you fear your spouse or family situation? Do you need to confide in a trusted peer or family counselor?

____

____

____

9. Are there blind spots in your marriage that are greatly affecting your family?

____

____

____

10. As a married couple, are you doing well at honoring and loving those who are single in your life?

____

____

____

11. When is the last time you verbally expressed love or intentionally appreciated each other for their hard work?

____

____

____

Day 13

Seeking Approval: Finding Identity in Something Else

Read: 1 Samuel 15, Galatians 1:6-12

This may be one of the most subtle brokenness topics within a family, yet could have overwhelming effects. Most would not even dream of associating the topic of "seeking approval" with broken families.

This topic might involve seeking any type of approval from within and outside the family. Maybe there's a child who is desperately seeking the approval of their mother or father. Or, a sibling is seeking the acceptance and approval of their other siblings. This could be a wife seeking the approval of a husband. It could be a husband seeking the approval of in-laws. It might be your family seeking the approval of neighbors or social elites. There could be varying degrees of people pleasing in terms of how much of your time and energy it demands.

While seeking approval might be subtle, it can lead to devastating effects. It can affect relationships through constant concern and worry, potentially leading someone to vastly alter their life and personality to fit into another person's mold.

There are mental health effects to seeking approval as well, from anxiety to suicidal ideation. Seeking approval could also lead to spending vast amounts of time and money on things and activities that don't bring you joy and aren't moving you towards God. Even more dangerous, it could lead you into compromising your faith and morals as you try to please others. The impact of seeking approval can be devastating to you and your family.

In the Bible, there was an ancient king who had it all. His people followed him and God was pleased with him. He won crucial victories for his kingdom with the help of God at his side. This man was the first anointed king of Israel, Saul.

As his reign continued however, Saul started to turn in a different direction as he started to seek the approval of man instead of obeying God. The first recorded instance of Saul seeking approval from others was when he was impatient in waiting on the Lord's favor when it came to battle. In his impatience, he initiated a burnt offering without priestly assistance which was not allowed by God. The prophet Samuel rebuked him for this in 1 Samuel 13.

In the second instance recorded, Saul received a command from God to completely destroy neighboring kingdoms. This might sound harsh, but these kingdoms sought to completely destroy the Israelites whom God had chosen. Remaining prisoners of war, intermarriage, and taking spoils could result in a thorn in Israel's side and take Israel's vision off the true God.

Instead, Saul spared the life of the enemy king and took spoils of sheep and cattle as a cheap means to produce burnt offerings to God. Saul then set up a monument in his own honor. After this second disobedience, here is part of the conversation between Saul and Samuel as found in 1 Samuel 15:20-26:

> *"But I did obey the LORD," Saul said. "I went on the mission the LORD assigned me. I completely destroyed*

the Amalekites and brought back Agag their king. The soldiers took sheep and cattle from the plunder, the best of what was devoted to God, in order to sacrifice them to the LORD your God at Gilgal."

But Samuel replied:

"Does the LORD delight in burnt offerings and sacrifices as much as in obeying the LORD?
To obey is better than sacrifice, and to heed is better than the fat of rams. For rebellion is like the sin of divination, and arrogance like the evil of idolatry. Because you have rejected the word of the LORD, he has rejected you as king."

Then Saul said to Samuel, "I have sinned. I violated the LORD's command and your instructions. I was afraid of the men and so I gave in to them. Now I beg you, forgive my sin and come back with me, so that I may worship the LORD."

But Samuel said to him, "I will not go back with you. You have rejected the word of the LORD, and the LORD has rejected you as king over Israel!"

Saul admits he disobeyed the Lord by giving in and pleasing the people around him. This was not an isolated case, but a developed pattern with Saul that didn't go well for him. He lost his influence, his kingdom, and eventually his life because of the direction it took him. God took His favor away from Saul and gave it to his successor, David, who not only respected Saul's kingship through the whole process, but gained the allegiance from the people. This not only angered Saul, but he sought to kill David and anyone who challenged his kingship. The downfall of Saul's life began with the constant pattern of people-pleasing and by doing so, consistent disobedience toward God.

Hope. If you are someone who struggles with pleasing others to the point that it consumes your time and energy, I hope this would be a wake-up call to turn from this brokenness before it impacts future generations.

The beautiful aspect of coming to faith in Christ is when it comes to seeking the approval of others, we don't have to work to earn the approval of God. If we are in Christ, we already have God's approval. When God sees us, He sees the perfection of His son Jesus who took the penalty our sin and is our new identity. That doesn't mean we are perfect, but our position in God's kingdom is secure. This isn't because of our works, but what Jesus did on the cross for us. Since we have God's approval, why would we need to labor to seek man's approval by possibly compromising our faith and morals just to please others? Paul issues a warning to the Galatian church on the topic of people pleasing in Galatians 1:10:

> *Am I now trying to win the approval of human beings, or of God? Or am I trying to please people? If I were still trying to please people, I would not be a servant of Christ.*

There is nothing wrong with trying to be at peace with family and friends, but are you changing who you are and what you believe to elevate the demands of people over what God desires? This is when a person ventures into the dangerous territory of people pleasing, similar to Saul.

Next steps. What are some next steps to help you and your family shift away from seeking other's approval, and focus on God instead? Here are some questions to help you journal and reflect:

1. As you read the story of Saul's downfall, how does your view on people pleasing within your family and among your peers and authority figures change?

   ____

   ____

   ____

2. What ways are you compromising your values and faith by seeking the approval of others?

   ____

   ____

   ____

3. Think of your childhood, teenage, and adult years. In what ways are you seeking the approval from your parents, and has that journey been compromising your faith in an unhealthy manner?

   ____

   ____

   ____

4. If you are a parent, are you creating an environment for your kids where they feel the urge to constantly earn your approval rather than knowing they are loved unconditionally?

   ____

   ____

   ____

5. Is there a peer or mentor in your life you feel safe asking about an honest self-assessment as to how you are doing when it comes to pleasing an audience of one (God), rather than seeking it in humankind?

____

____

____

6. If you have committed your life to Christ, do you know you are loved unconditionally by God and don't need to seek the approval of God?

____

____

____

7. Now you are in a relationship with God and are growing closer to Him through sanctification, what can you shift in your life to please God?

____

____

____

8. If you are constantly trying to people-please and can't stop, what are your fears in turning from it? What is the root of your addiction to seek the approval of others?

____

____

____

Day 14

Mental Health: Brokenness of the Mind

Read: 2 Corinthians 12:7-10, 1 Thessalonians 4:13-18

Years ago, the topic of mental health was so taboo, people rarely talked about it or addressed it unless it turned into a major issue. Seeing a counselor used to indicate there was something incredibly wrong with you. I can remember meeting with a counselor in elementary school for a short period of time to address anger issues. Even in 5th grade, I would have been devastated if any of my peers discovered I was seeing a counselor.

For better and for worse, things have changed in our culture. For better, mental health issues are no longer taboo like they were in the past. Many people are forward with how they are struggling mentally as we learn more about the hereditary and environmental causes of such issues.

For worse, mental health flare-ups have skyrocketed within families in the last decade, especially among young people. From anxiety to emotional instability to depression and suicidal ideation, most people know at least someone who struggles with mental health.

According to the National Alliance on Mental Health:

- One-fifth of U.S. adults experience mental health illness each year
- One-sixth of U.S. youth aged 6-17 experience a mental health disorder each year

- 50% of all lifetime mental illness begins by age 14, and 75% by age 24
- Suicide is the 2nd leading cause of death among children aged 10-14

Chances are very high that within a family, especially one that experiences brokenness in relationships, someone struggles with mental health.

Hope. The Bible doesn't speak directly on the topic of mental health, but scripture does talk about the brokenness plaguing the heart, mind, and soul. Scripture reveals that God is ultimately the one who renews the mind (Romans 12:2), gives us peace (John 14:27), and gives us rest in Him (Matthew 11:28-30).

There are certainly biblical characters who showed signs of mental health-related issues. As Elijah feared Queen Jezebel, he fled and isolated to the point of wishing death upon himself. This was the point when God met him and gave him encouragement (1 Kings 19). Jonah reluctantly preached repentance to the Ninevites and then sulked in a depressive state while eventually wishing death upon himself after God showed the Ninevites mercy (Jonah 4). Spiritual forces had an effect on King Saul's mental well-being as an evil spirit tormented Saul (1 Samuel 16). Even Jesus cast a demon out of a man from the Gerasenes and afterwards it was recorded that this man was now "in his right mind" (Mark 5:15).

Similar to examples in scripture, there are many reasons a person might not be mentally healthy today. There may be one or many different internal and external forces at work in someone struggling with mental health. A grave mistake would be to take a simplistic approach and label someone's mental health condition as a result of just one issue. There might be a combination of many factors or unrevealed spiritual forces at work. It's a mistake to assume sin directly contributes to a mental health condition, or to assert sin is not a contributing factor at all. There may be a host of contributing factors and sin might be one of those.

In the case of Jonah, we see his hardened heart contributing to his desire to die. Yet, with the Gerasene man who Jesus healed, we see the external spiritual factor playing a lead role. Mental health issues should be addressed on a case-by-case basis, seeking to understand the many underlying factors.

If you have a family member or close friend who struggles with mental health related issues, sometimes the best approach is to seek understanding by coming alongside them in their struggles. Sometimes, we create barriers by unintentionally saying hurtful things such as:

- "You just need to get over that anxiety"
- "Why don't you just try having fun when you feel down or depressed?"
- "Why don't you see someone and get some medication?"
- "Why don't you turn from the sin of _____ so that you can be healed of this?"

Remember sometimes we don't know all the details or extent of the mental health issue someone is struggling with. Some people may even be good at suppressing and hiding the full picture of what they are going through.

The last piece of hope is based on what I have heard from those who have gone through serious mental health issues and have gained a wonderful biblical perspective on it. God might not heal you. This might not seem hopeful or biblical to you, but is it possible that you are harboring a western misconception of God and healing? The apostle Paul pleaded with God to take away a metaphorical thorn in his side. We don't know what this affliction was, but this is what God taught Paul when He didn't take away this thorn in 2 Corinthians 12:7-10:

> *Therefore, in order to keep me from becoming conceited, I was given a thorn in my flesh, a messenger of Satan, to torment me. Three times I pleaded with the Lord to take it away from me. But he said to me, "My grace is sufficient for you, for my power is made perfect in weakness." Therefore I will boast all the more gladly about my weaknesses, so that Christ's power may rest on me. That is why, for Christ's sake, I delight in weaknesses, in insults, in hardships, in persecutions, in difficulties. For when I am weak, then I am strong.*

We don't know why God chooses to heal certain people and not others, but regardless, we ought to rejoice in our weaknesses and humility. That is where God's grace is sufficient and Christ's power can reign in us. Prayerfully, as you grow in Christ, you will see victory over sin and temptation. Ultimately, we will not be free from the effects of the Fall until Christ returns and makes all things new, including your body and mind. Our hope does not rely on science, medicine, psychiatry, or positive thinking, rather, our ultimate hope is in the resurrection when Christ returns and makes all things new.

Please don't hear me saying that we should ignore medical attention. If you are struggling with mental health issues as a Christian and are debating seeking psychological or medical attention, it's very important to know that by choosing clinical help, we don't trust God any less. I believe you can bridge both the clinical and spiritual world to not only help yourself psychologically, but also use biblical principles to utilize the resources God has provided such as counseling and medication. Please don't let a faulty perception that "seeking medical treatment is not trusting God" be a barrier to getting the help you need. In the same way we utilize a hospital for physical injuries or a counselor for marriage issues, we are not trusting God any less. Perhaps seeking medical attention for mental health issues is the next step in trusting God to provide.

Next steps. Here are some questions to ponder as you reflect on mental health within your family:

1. If you are a parent with a child struggling with mental health, are you seeking to understand their condition or brushing it off as just a phase?

   ____

   ____

   ____

2. If you are struggling with mental health, what external and internal factors are contributing to it? What is the appropriate next step?

   ____

   ____

   ____

3. Are you trusting God with your mental health? Rather than just saying it with your mouth, are you sincerely trusting God?

____

____

____

4. When you read about Paul's thorn not being taken away and God's grace is sufficient for him, have you thought of the parallels with your mental health?

____

____

____

5. If you struggle with mental health, is your hope in Christ's return and the resurrection? Again, rather than just believing this intellectually, is your mindset and life impacted by the hope of the resurrection? Perhaps you need to dwell on the encouragement in 1 Thessalonians 4:13-18.

____

____

____

6. If your mental health is affecting your daily life and the lives of others, have you or family members sought professional help to determine the internal and external contributing factors? Have you considered medication to help with the process?

____

____

____

7. If you have family, friends, coworkers, or colleagues who have been affected by your mental health, have you appropriately addressed it with them to let them in on what you are struggling with so they have understanding and know how they can help?

____

____

____

8. Is there sin you need to address and turn from, which may contribute to a mental health issue?

____

____

____

Day 15

Disabled: Brokenness of the Mind and Body

Read: John 9

As we've addressed various issues of brokenness within families, much of it has derived from family or individual sin. There are other aspects of family brokenness simply resulting from living in a broken and fallen world. One of these topics are physical and mental disabilities.

It's important to note here: a physical or mental disability is a matter of degree. A person who has poor vision or imperfect teeth might have a physical disability, but this pales in comparison to the degree by which some people experience disabilities that do not allow them to see, hear, walk, or talk. Not all disabilities are created equal.

If you are not physically disabled, chances are you know someone who is. Maybe even someone in your family has a disability that has caused you or others to adjust how you live and function. Most western individualists are generally uncomfortable or have immense pity for those with physical or mental disabilities.

Hope. Many Christians are challenged theologically by the existence of difficult disabilities. The age-old questions of the "problem of pain" or the "problem of evil" begin to surface as they wrestle with the existence of an all-powerful loving God in the midst of such pain and suffering. In fact, it is much easier for us to think in simplistic terms such as this family or person sinned greatly, therefore they are afflicted with this or that consequence. Another example would assume if this person or family would just believe harder, God would heal them. However, that is a simplistic view even Jesus rebuked in John 9:1-7:

> *As he went along, he saw a man blind from birth. His disciples asked him, "Rabbi, who sinned, this man or his parents, that he was born blind?"*
>
> *"Neither this man nor his parents sinned," said Jesus, "but this happened so that the works of God might be displayed in him. As long as it is day, we must do the works of him who sent me. Night is coming, when no one can work. While I am in the world, I am the light of the world."*
>
> *After saying this, he spit on the ground, made some mud with the saliva, and put it on the man's eyes. "Go," he told him, "wash in the Pool of Siloam" (this word means "Sent"). So the man went and washed, and came home seeing.*

Jesus not only affirms this man's blindness wasn't due to him or his parents having a lack of belief or a grave sin, but the works of God might be displayed in him. In fact, later in John 9, Jesus uses the example of healing the blind man to show the very people who proclaimed to have insight and knowledge about God's kingdom were the very people who were spiritually blind. There are other instances where Jesus heals and even raises from the dead so the glory of God may be shown.

As mentioned in previous devotions, this doesn't always mean that God will heal you in this lifetime. We don't fully know how and why He heals some, but not others.

I want you to hear from a friend of mine who prayed for healing from the disability of Spina Bifida. After years, this is what she wrestled through: "God chose not to heal me physically, but He very much healed me emotionally and spiritually. I used to feel very angry and betrayed by God for not taking away my Spina Bifida, until I realized that what I needed was spiritual healing and emotional healing to desire God's plan in life rather than what I wanted in life. Just because I didn't get my way, doesn't mean I didn't get the healing I needed." She now works at a faith-based clinic that offers counseling services for a variety health related issues. She's also discovered God's grace is sufficient and made perfect amidst her physical weakness.

Ultimately, there is hope in the resurrection when Christ returns. One thing I've noticed in being around those with mental and physical disabilities, there doesn't tend to be sorrow and mourning like I would anticipate. Perhaps many with disabilities who know Jesus have a solid mindset of the hope they hold onto with Christ. Perhaps because of their disabilities, they are less enamored by the idols of the world like many able-bodied individuals and therefore have clearer hope in God. Perhaps they are able to see Christ and eternity so clearly amidst their physical condition. Perhaps we who are not disabled can learn a lot from the meek and mild faith of those who are disabled.

Henri J.M. Nouwen was an ordained priest and author who had a distinguished teaching career at Yale, Harvard, and Notre Dame. Yet, he was impacted the most when he accepted a position at L'Arche Daybreak, a community for people with intellectual disabilities in Ontario. Nouwen said it was there he found the community he was searching for his entire life. He remained there until his death. He learned more about the love and compassion of Christ through those whom our culture would call weak. Would we approach a mentally and physically disabled person with the same kingdom mindset?

Next steps. Here are some questions to help you reflect on the brokenness of physical and intellectual disabilities:

1. If there are such disabilities in your family, what are you doing to show the care and compassion needed?

   ____

   ____

   ____

2. Do you have a skewed perception of disabilities when it comes to sin, healing, and lack of belief?

   ____

   ____

   ____

3. What can you do to love on other families or friends that have mental or physical disabilities in their families?

   ____

   ____

   ____

4. How has your perception of strength and weakness in God's kingdom versus this world changed?

   ____

   ____

   ____

5. When you think of idols and worldly pleasures being stripped away which allows you to see Christ more clearly, how might that cause you to adjust your goals and priorities in life?

____

____

____

6. What is keeping you from seeing the hope of eternity and the hope of resurrection at Christ's return?

____

____

____

7. In what ways is your church or ministry being open and accommodating to those who struggle with mental or physical disabilities?

____

____

____

Day 16

Substance Abuse: Brokenness of Addiction

Read: 1 Corinthians 6:19-20, Ephesians 5:18, 1 Corinthians 10:23-24

We all know families where substance abuse through drugs or alcohol has been a struggle. It might even affect your family. One of the reasons this topic can be so challenging is because we are constantly wondering where the line is between acceptable and abuse. Oftentimes there is also a strong connection between deeper mental health issues and substance abuse.

To add to the complexity, there are some substances that are legal to utilize, such as alcohol or drugs. Other substances are very dangerous, illegal, and carry great consequences in addition to addiction. Then, there are those who would even argue substance abuse could be as simple as addictions to caffeine or sugar. While all these claims are true, we are going to focus on substance abuse that impacts families. Where is the line with family members? How do we know when someone has crossed that line?

Without thinking critically, the question of what constitutes substance abuse may be hard to answer. However, many definitely know when things cross into abuse. Some families have struggled for years with a relative's addiction to alcohol or drugs and how it's affected them. Sadly, I've seen some children who were basically raised at the local bar as their parents were addicted to alcohol through their childhood. I once saw someone post a hypothetical challenge on social media asking, “Could you give up alcohol for a year for $1 million?” This person responded with an emphatic no, which I thought this was rather comical. However, it shows the sad reality of the level of addiction existing today.

Hope. While the Bible doesn’t speak directly to drug use, and it sparingly mentions alcohol, scripture does address the heart of the issue. In fact, in regard to alcohol, Christians have argued about the permission or prohibition given to drinking as there are many scriptures advocating for and against alcohol. Paul recommends his disciple drink wine for his stomach ailments (1 Timothy 5:23). Psalm 104 praises God for wine which gladdens the heart of man. Jesus’ first miracle is turning water into wine and He uses wine at the Last Supper as a symbol of His blood shed for sin. However, there are many areas of scripture condemning drunkards and calling out woes upon those who indulge in drinking (Galatians 5:21, Proverbs 23, Hosea 4:11). How then are we to approach such substances that can cause addiction?

We are constantly asking if we should drink or not, or if we should take a substance or not. This has caused Christians to swing hard in either the direction of legalism or licentiousness. Legalism would assert opposition against all substances including legal ones, which can create a pompous and rule-based rigidity. Whereas when the pendulum is swung hard in the other direction, licentious people throw away the rules and claim freedom to engage in a variety of substances, leading to the great temptation of addiction. Some then try to meet somewhere in the middle proclaiming “moderation”, but even that doesn’t fully answer the biblical approach to substances.

Perhaps we are asking the wrong questions. Rather than focusing on the substance itself, maybe we should be asking ourselves these two questions:

1. What has influence over you?
2. We may have the right to engage in this substance, but does that mean we should engage?

Principle one: What has influence over you? Ephesians 5:18 is a simple yet profound verse on influence:

> *Do not be drunk on wine, but be filled with the Spirit.*

At first, this seems like a strange contrast with very different subjects, until you understand what the author is aiming at. As Christians, we believe the Holy Spirit lives within us and has tremendous influence over us. Scripture is constantly pushing us toward submitting and trusting in the Holy Spirit's influence.

However, alcohol, opioids, prescription drugs, recreational drugs, and hard drugs can also have tremendous influence over us. Without realizing it, these substances can influence our thoughts and actions. If we're not careful, substances will influence and change the way we live and interact with others and God.

Principle two: We may have the right to engage in this substance, but does that mean we should engage? Our western culture values freedom and self-autonomy. We are quick to exclaim our rights, even if it adversely affects others. Scripture addresses this complexity in 1 Corinthians 10:23-24 by stating:

> *"I have the right to do anything," you say – but not everything is beneficial. "I have the right to do anything" – but not everything is constructive. No one should seek their own good, but the good of others.*

Paul here is specifically addressing the complicated topic of eating meat that has been sacrificed to idols, but out of this issue comes a powerful principle. When we think of engaging in any activity, we are prone to be thinking about our satisfaction and pleasure, rather than the lives of those around us. We are so consumed with an individualistic mindset that we fail to realize how our actions impact others. It may be wise for you to sacrifice your rights in order to love and do good to others. You may have to start thinking about how your actions with substances affect others, rather than your own fulfillment.

These two principles might not provide all the answers to substance use, but they do give clear principles as to how we ought to approach any issue.

Notice also how these two principles reflect the Greatest Commandment that Jesus shared in Matthew 22:37-40:

> *"'Love the Lord your God with all your heart and with all your soul and with all your mind.' This is the first and greatest commandment. And the second is like it: 'Love your neighbor as yourself.' All the Law and the Prophets hang on these two commandments."*

All other laws and direction related to food, time, money, lifestyle, family direction, and more, ought to flow through these two commands, including our approach to substances.

Next steps. Whether substance abuse affects you, your own family, others, or even if you are determining if you have a problem with substances, here are some reflection questions to help you journal.

These are questions related to substances that are legal, but could be abused:

1. How often do you drink alcohol or use other substances? Are there times where you "need" this?

   ____

   ____

   ____

2. Are you using substances to medicate pain, hurt, or voids in your life?

   ____

   ____

   ____

3. If you have a hard time determining if alcohol, medications, opioids, or recreation drugs have become an issue, could you go six months without them?

   ____

   ____

   ____

4. Have you thought about who is around you when you drink? Does it tarnish your influence for Christ in their lives?

   ____

   ____

   ____

5. Do you have a list of practical guidelines when it comes to legal substances to prevent them from taking influence over you or to prevent others from falling into sin themselves?

____

____

____

6. Have you taken a strong legalistic approach or licentious approach on legal substances? Do you need to soften your stance?

____

____

____

7. Are you respecting the laws of your state or country when it comes to substances?

____

____

____

8. Has your use of substances tarnished relationships with friends or family? Do you become anxious, angry, or violent?

____

____

____

9. Do you have a close relative who struggles with substance abuse that you could either confront or seek professional help? (If you fear for your safety related to a relative's substance abuse, please discretely contact local authorities or a professional counselor.)

____

____

____

Here are some questions related to illegal substance use and abuse:

1. If you are a person who uses illegal substances, have you thought about reaching out and getting professional help?

   ____

   ____

   ____

2. In what ways has your illegal substance usage affected relationships with your friends and family?

   ____

   ____

   ____

3. Are you letting these substances influence your life and affect those around you?

   ____

   ____

   ____

4. Have you considered the chain reaction of crime and drug money that goes into your illegal substances?

   ____

   ____

   ____

5. Do you have a close relative who struggles with abuse with illegal substances that you could come alongside with or seek professional help? (If you worry about your safety related to a relative's illegal substance abuse, please discretely reach out to local authorities or licensed counselors now.)

   ____

   ____

   ____

Conclusion

By now, I hope the level of brokenness in every family is evident. Too often, we assume other families have it all together, but it's rarely the case. Families can put on a great show, but behind those masks there is a degree of brokenness to all.

Thankfully, that is not where the story ends. The purpose of Christ's coming was not just to die for your sins so you can be with Him in Heaven. Christ died to reconcile all things to Himself. This includes reconciling broken creation, animosity between ethnic groups, divisions between races and nations, and mending broken relationships within families. The Christian life is difficult because it means stepping out of the comfort of this world to do the hard work of reconciliation as stated in 2 Corinthians 5:18-20:

> *All this is from God, who reconciled us to himself through Christ and gave us the ministry of reconciliation: that God was reconciling the world to himself in Christ, not counting people's sins against them. And he has committed to us the message of reconciliation. We are therefore Christ's ambassadors, as though God were making his appeal through us. We implore you on Christ's behalf: Be reconciled to God.*

The Christian life was not meant to be an individual endeavor of only reconciliation between you and God. It's a collective effort of seeing restoration now in relationships as God originally intended before the Fall. He entrusts this mission of restoring relationships to you.

Acknowledgments

When I think of the people who helped me put together this devotional and first published book, many colleagues, coworkers, and family come to mind.

I certainly could not have created the content through personal experience alone. Thank you to Dani for offering me your thoughts on many of the chapters from your own growth and experience. To Meghan who came alongside and help me copyedit this devotional.

I am also grateful for several Cru staff. To Amy, who published a book herself and helped me through the process of becoming published. To Scott, who continued to encourage me to produce something utilizing the growth I've experienced from a broken home to help impact others as they confront the effects of their past.

A very special thanks goes out to family who have been with me during even the hardest aspects of family brokenness. Even while mistakes were made, I never doubted you cared for me. Thank you, Leah, who was kind enough to read through the manuscript to ensure I fairly shared my personal experiences while respecting and honoring all of my family members.

Finally, I thank my King and Savior Jesus Christ who not only forgave my sin and took away my shame and guilt, but taught me how to love others. My identity is solely in Him, not the brokenness of my past.

www.ingramcontent.com/pod-product-compliance
Lightning Source LLC
LaVergne TN
LVHW020649100826
845148LV00012B/2399

* 9 7 9 8 2 1 8 9 5 7 5 1 3 *